PUPPY TRAINING

Proven And Fast Working Techniques To Train Your Puppy In Obedience, Potty Training And Crate Training

Robert Mattews & Marilyn Willows

Table of Contents

Introduction

Chances are you have heard of Puppy Training. Most people have. However, the kind of puppy training many people have in mind is where you get to show your puppy what the parameters of your homestead are, so that the puppy doesn't stray into your neighbor's compound or onto public property. While it's good for your puppy to know the limitations of the home compound, what this book endeavors to explain is the full training a puppy needs in order to mix with people and other puppies in a decent fashion. When you train your puppy in the manner explained in this guide, you will be a proud puppy owner because your puppy will obey your instructions at the first sign; move away to pee or poop at the designated place; alert you about its wish to relieve itself if you are away from home; and generally behave in a civilized way.

Again, in this era of suits and counter suits in courts of law, you can't afford to have a dog that barks and bites at will. Remember public nuisance is enough to take you before a judge and get some sizeable dollar fine slapped on you if someone engages a good lawyer, particularly one averse to dogs. And, you, obviously, don't want to imagine what would happen if you were sued because your dog bit someone. You could spend years in jail!

For that reason, this puppy training guide is a must have, especially considering how simple and direct its tips are, and how real its examples are as well. Besides, after reading this book, you'll realize that you really don't have to be a formally trained puppy trainer to train your puppy effectively.

Happy reading and best wishes in your puppy training experience!

Chapter 1: Important Puppy Development Phases

And what puppy are we talking about here, you think? Yes – a young dog. It's important to be clear from the onset, knowing how dynamic language is. Don't think, for instance, that humans always shared their young ones with goats – no! *Kid* is a later development – in fact developed in the early years of the 19th century – as language evolved. So, there – you can't take anything for granted.

Now you may know dogs to have very cool young ones, looking all docile and loveable; and you are right. The only thing you may not know is that in their early days, around three weeks of age, the puppies do not engage their brain. Whatever dogs think about, if they do weigh issues at all, these tiny ones do not in their first 20 days – as in, they don't engage their brain at all.

Mh – how's that possible when we see them doing things like eating; like seeking out their mother; like sleeping...? Yes, they do all that alright, but guess what...? It's some kind of automated response to an urge. They react by eating when they sense hunger, sleep when exhaustion and the urge to sleep overwhelms them, lie snugly next to their mother when they yearn for mother love; that's it – no contemplations, reasoning and stuff. For that reason, you need to handle your puppies with utmost care in their first three weeks.

How to handle your puppies in their first 3wks:

Care for the mother dog the best way possible

The reason for this is that the puppies will be depending on their mother almost entirely during those first three weeks when they can't tell danger from safety; or enemy from friend. A well fed and comfortable mother has the ability and inclination to care for its young ones as opposed to a dog that is worried whether it'll ever get fed and so on.

Prepare a convenient place for the mother

A nursing bitch is not like any other dog when it comes to its resting place. This one needs a place that is not only comfortable to lie – sometimes with its puppies – but also one that is secluded. A nursing dog values its privacy. So, if you were used to staying with your dog in the living room, don't reason that the area is still large enough for all of you, including the puppies. The mother needs a private place. And since it's the main caregiver besides you, it is necessary that you make it convenient for it to make the puppies comfortable.

Give your puppies hands-on support at least once

It is not enough that the puppies are suckling their mother and that you are feeding the mother well. While those are important factors, it is important that you visit the puppies two times in a day – or at least once – to observe them and ensure they are doing fine. Remember the puppies can't speak out and wouldn't even know how to communicate like their mother because... – yes, their brains are not yet at work!

Weigh your puppies every day

If you recall (believing you knew it, in the first place...), dogs are mammals. And some of the things that humans do to their babies in taking care of them apply to other mammals too – like dogs. The same way it is important to weigh babies, the same way it is to weigh puppies. In most cases, for example, there is a correlation between the weight of the young one and its health. So, the gradual increment of the puppy's weight cannot be underrated.

Let the puppies remain in the whelping box

Puppies are loveable and you may wish to show them off to friends or begin molding them into what you'd like them to be – yes, when they grow up – but no; this is not the time for that. Unless they initiate the walk around, let them remain comfortably in that whelping box you made for them before they were delivered. That is what is expected of them in their first delicate 20 days of their lives.

How to handle your puppies between 3wks and 4wks

What you begin to notice by the twenty-first day of your puppies' lives is a set of new creatures, with a sense of life you never noticed before. It is now, more than ever before, that you begin to appreciate the presence of new beings in your family. It doesn't matter what breed it is – a Labrador, a Bulldog, a German Shepherd, name it – they all begin to exhibit a zest for life after three weeks. Every sense that you can associate with mammals is right there; smelling, hearing, and all the rest.

So is that a sign they are independent?

The answer is an emphatic no! The fact that their senses are well aroused at this time means that the puppies can somehow distinguish you from their mother. And that means, they hold their mother in higher esteem (than you, yes), and they have an extra strong bond with her. Every time she gets up to walk away from their whelping box they are concerned about where she is headed to. In fact, between this period of between three and four weeks, the puppies develop a very high level of awareness; being very conscious of their surroundings.

To sum up the sensitivity of this stage in a puppy's life, let's just say that it would be the worst time for a puppy to lose its mother. It is the stage during which the puppy's emotional development is at its most intense and you cannot afford to destabilize it in any way. In fact, considering that it is the period during which the puppy has become self conscious, you can see how easy it is to make an impression on it. Even various emotions will be impacted at this time; and they had better be impacted positively. Depending on its experiences at this stage in life, the puppy can grow to be a shy dog or one that fears everyone. Its emotional growth takes place at this time, and so, whatever traits it learns now, are likely to form part of its personal character.

During this period, the puppy even gets curious about what the mother is doing and what you are putting in the area around it. For that reason, it is advisable that you create some space beside the puppies' whelping box, and make it some form of potty zone.

How to handle your puppies between Day 29 and Day 49

As you may well suspect, the puppies can't wait to venture

out. Their sense of smell make them curious as to what they are cooking out there, their sense of hearing makes them wonder who the heck is making the noises they hear, and there is generally the wish to do what the mother is doing – and that is, being more mobile.

In short, after four weeks of hanging around the whelping box, the puppies want to explore beyond that area. Dog experts say, do not restrain them. In fact, encourage them to visit the living room and wherever else people are doing their activities. In fact, isn't that how they learn how to relate with the people in the home? And you need not worry about them getting lost – the tiny animals won't stray far. After all, their sense of security tells them they need to be within familiar grounds. So, they'll explore within a safe perimeter.

How do you help the puppies at this stage?

Well, you've got a role alright. Apart from allowing wandering around and encouraging them to visit other areas of the house beyond their whelping box zone, you can consciously expand their play area. At the same time you can stop confining their eating place to the whelping box or the area around it. By doing this, you'll be helping the puppies to integrate with your family members, and also to familiarize themselves with the environment. And if you pause to think about it critically, is there a better way a puppy can learn the likes and dislikes of human beings than living amidst them?

The long and short of it is this: let the poor things mingle with you; go to where life is taking place. This is not the time to relocate your curious puppies to the garage, for peace sake! They won't be destructive if you pay attention to them. In fact, they are like little children – curious; that's it. Any damage that happens to property, if any, is accidental. So, again, do not succumb to any temptation to put those puppies in some back room; or to dispatch them to the barn. For them to learn, and learn well, and to develop all their faculties well, they need to be in a regular living environment.

How can you tell the puppies are learning?

It is pretty easy to tell that your puppies are learning. For one, you will find them responding to sounds; to people's voices; and they actually show signs of recognizing various people as they get used to them. It's just like children, right? And something else – hierarchy! Yes, your puppies do begin to develop some sort of pecking order amongst themselves. And so you'll be able to tell those with strong personalities from those that are somewhat shy or reserved. You can tell that because as you watch them, you'll notice that there are those who'll almost always be leading in activity, including feeding, and those who'll be following suit.

How to keep your puppies' behavior within acceptable range

Well, you've seen that the strong ones are beginning to show and the weak ones too are becoming identifiable. Domination and being subdued are natural developments. And as much as such developments are natural, your home is no jungle. So the rule of the jungle shouldn't be allowed to prevail here; you can't allow it. That means this is not the time to say that only the strong survive. You want to keep things under control where puppy care is concerned.

Essentially what we are saying is, yes, your puppies need to socialize, they need to explore their environment, they need an opportunity to experiment with their senses; but you need to protect those that seem vulnerable. You need to be keen and if you notice a bully amongst your puppies, make it clear to such a puppy that certain behavior, especially bullying, is not acceptable. And when it's time to place any of the puppies for adoption, begin with the bully. Note: it's not because you despise the poor bully, it knows no better after all. Only that if you keep it around for long, it's bound to affect the personality of other docile puppies negatively.

So what are the highlights of this stage?

- Well, this is the period during which you learn the personalities of your different puppies. This is important because you can only decide with close accuracy the appropriate home for your puppy if you understand its likes and dislikes; its strengths and weaknesses; and its characteristics in general.

- This is the stage where your puppy develops social skills – playing, sharing, and so on – by living amongst other puppies; with all its senses developing as they should. In fact, it is the stage where the puppy learns and practices to be competitive.

- It is the stage where you get to learn the puppy that is great in associating with others and one that needs to be set aside by way of quick adoption, in order not to destabilize the development of other puppies.

At this juncture, it is important to point out that not all puppies are ready to be separated from their mother or to be weaned at the same age. Whether or not a puppy is ready for adoption at a certain age mainly depends on its breed.

How to handle your puppies after 7 weeks

After a good 49 days, you can say with certainty than your puppies are emotionally developed. And with stable emotions, it then becomes easy for you, or whoever else is put in charge, to train them. So, if you've been wondering what the best time to begin training your puppy is, seven weeks is it. Still, you need to appreciate that the puppy's brain is still not as developed as that of an adult dog; it is still actually developing at this age. But the puppy is capable of learning.

So, how do you handle the puppy at this stage?

Well, begin your puppy crate training. Just in case you didn't know it, teaching becomes more effective with consistency.

In this case, therefore:

- You need to engage in crate training for sessions lasting an hour or two every day

- You need to have two puppies in each crate during this period

And suppose there is no shortage of crates? Maybe that question has cropped up in your mind. However, the principle of putting two puppies in each crate is not adopted because of shortage of crates or even space. It is advised because the puppies have just gotten out of the communal care, where they were allowed to lie and snuggle close to one another, and where they followed their mother at will. As such, you don't want these young ones to experience some kind of shock that may be occasioned by drastic change of lifestyle. The transition from mother care to independent existence needs to be smooth and one way of enhancing that smoothness is having at least two puppies giving each other company. That way, none of them suffers anxiety as they learn to leave crowds behind.

In fact, a week of 2-puppy company is enough for the puppy

to develop relative independence. And in 8wks, you can put each puppy in its own crate without negative reaction from the puppy. In essence, therefore, your puppy is ready to be dispatched to a new environment – a new home – at the age of eight weeks.

Does one have to wait for a whole 8wks before giving a puppy away?

Oh yes! It is necessary to care for your puppy for some duration of not less than 2mths before you give it for adoption because there is no substitute that can equal the puppy's mother. You see, you can be very good with dogs and puppies, but you can't bark. These puppies need to comprehend the barking language; and at that early age, they can only learn it from the mother. And, of course, there are other mannerisms that the puppy is going to learn from the mother, which you may not even have an idea about. Who knows what the mother dog says to its young one when you are warning your child against poking a finger in its nose?

The point is, even dogs have etiquette; and you need to allow the mother ample time to teach its young one how to behave in different circumstances; how to be respectful; and, let's say, many other social skills. Very often, you may be able to identify a dog that skipped this nurturing stage by its behavior when it's all grown up – often not pleasant.

What happens when the puppy is between 7wks and 12wks?

Do you have something to teach your puppy? Many would ask in response, why not? There's definitely, a way you'd like your dog to behave just the same way you'd expect anyone living with you to behave in a certain way. There are boundaries not to be crossed, routines not to be missed, and so on. This age when the puppy has just been weaned and before it can qualify as an adult is the best time to teach whatever you consider important in a dog. If you do your teaching when your puppy is this age, you can be sure it will retain that behavior up to eternity. So, whatever personality you would like to see in a dog, begin creating it Day 50 of the puppy's age.

Aren't mothers possessive when you want to take their puppy away?

Oh, believe me, dog mothers want the puppies out of their way by the time they are seven weeks. So, you'll just be doing them a favor. And this shouldn't be strange, anyway, considering that by this age, the puppy has acquired some teeth. So it's good reasoning that the mother dog pushes these puppies away to live independently.

And again, if you let puppies remain with their mothers for too long, they'll be as deficient as the teenagers who live with their parents beyond leave-by date, so to speak. For one, the emotional development they had developed begins to get interfered with by the factor of dependence. So, the puppies become so used to relying on their mother that it becomes difficult for them to let go even when they have become mature dogs. And that is the same case that happens when you let puppies live together for too long. None of them really develops emotional independence.

So what is important, therefore, is:

- To have the puppies get their first shots between the ages of 7½ to 8 weeks

- To have the puppies receive their second shots at the age of 12 weeks

Optimum age to adopt a puppy

The ideal time to adopt a puppy is between 8wks and 9wks; with more emphasis being put on 9wks. By this age, the puppy will have become emotionally developed and stable; reasonably independent; and will have had its first jab. The reason you don't want to wait much longer is that as the person adopting the puppy, there's likely to be some mannerisms you'd like the puppy to learn, and some routines you'd like it to adopt, which are unique to the needs of your home or even your lifestyle.

And if you adopt a puppy when it is beyond 12wks of age, it's likely to have learnt some behavior that you may not necessarily be comfortable with, and which you cannot, at this stage, manage to change. All the same, in reality, many people adopt puppies from the time the puppies are 8wks up to the time they are 11wks of age. The only luck you may have when you adopt a puppy beyond 12wks of age is if the breeder to the initiative to socialize the puppy independently; that is away from the other puppies.

How should you treat a new puppy?

Once you adopt a new puppy, just treat it the way you would if it had been born in your homestead. In this case, you need to have the right information about its shots – the exact time the puppy received its first shot. And then you'll, of course, ensure it receives its second shot in a timely manner.

Make a point of introducing your newly adopted puppy to the people around you. And get into the habit of taking it for a walk.

A word of caution where walks are concerned:

Whenever you take your puppy for a walk, keep to the pavement; avoiding dirt roads and grass areas, until the puppy receives its second shot. Remember your puppy's health, just like that of a child, is of utmost importance.

And now, as this stage comes to an end, your puppy is ready to train in a kindergarten, if you so desire.

Chapter 2: What Do They Teach In A Puppy Kindergarten?

Well, an educated guess would have it that they teach the fundamentals of life in a puppy kindergarten. That's because the class is designed to begin when the puppies are of the ages ranging from 12wks to 18wks. What that then tells you is that these puppies will already have learnt basic mannerisms and conduct, including potty training and so on.

However, to be more specific, a puppy kindergarten demands that you and your puppy register for an educational class that equips you in positive puppy training. Here you will learn what to do in order to keep your experience with your puppy exciting even when it is challenging. You will also learn the luring skills that you can use on your puppy, in order to shape its behavior in a positive way. Puppy training can be challenging, but in a puppy kindergarten you'll learn how to cultivate good manners in your puppy and do it in a fun way.

How long are puppy kindergarten classes?

Puppy kindergarten classes are manageable even for people with busy lives. Usually you are expected to bring your puppy to class once every week, for a 1hr session; and mostly it's in the evening. Here you gather the skills that you are going to practice at home, and whose success can be observed during the following session in class. At home you are expected to practice what you've learnt in class several times in a day. That ensures that you and the puppy do not forget what you learnt and instead ingrain the behavior in you.

Can anyone else besides the puppy owner accompany the puppy?

Sure – most puppy kindergartens allow you to bring someone else who is also close to the puppy, especially a member of your family; but one person is required to be consistent as the puppy trainer in the kindergarten training sessions. If the member of your family you are bringing to the kindergarten class is a child, it is advised that the child be of 12yrs of age, if not over. And you are not, under any circumstances, allowed to send your puppy with a child alone to the training sessions. Handling an animal, no matter how tiny, carries some degree of risk, and no kindergarten wants to take too much responsibility besides puppy training.

The main idea of a kindergarten class is to enable a puppy owner develop a working relationship with his or her puppy, so that at the end of the day, life at home can be rewarding and enjoyable with the now well behaved puppy as part of the family.

The precious skills that your puppy acquires in a puppy kindergarten include:

- How to observe your actions and body language when the situation becomes distracting or even scary

- How to be cool when held on a leash and walk politely

- How to respond fast when you call

- How to respond instantly to a *sit* or *stay* command

- How to respond to the *wait* command

- How to differentiate the *wait* command from the *stay* command

- How to execute the command to go to an identified location

- How to execute the command to lie down at a specified location

- How to do particular tricks, e.g. responding to the command, *wipe paws*

While still at the kindergarten, your puppy gets to learn how to play certain games that are a confidence booster. Such games also help in your puppy's physical co-ordination. Some games also involve using equipment, e.g. stairs; the tunnel; ladder; and others. The puppy also learns to use cushions for balancing. In addition, your puppy is introduced to a variety of surfaces, and it leaves the kindergarten behaving like a well exposed dog. That exposure, consequently, makes it easy to socialize your puppy in different environments.

It is in the puppy kindergarten too that your puppy is introduced to different sights, so that once you are out in social life, the puppy doesn't get uncomfortable or behave in a way that can embarrass you. Of great advantage too is the aspect of sharing experiences, where you get to discuss the behavior of your puppy breed as you listen to other puppy owners disclose also what they know about their puppy breed.

Chapter 3: How to Develop a Lovely, Confident Puppy

Do you think that good DNA is all you need to have a puppy full of confidence and an aura of authority? Cancel that if you thought so. The environment can enhance your puppy's confidence and it also has room to erode it. As a puppy owner, therefore, it is your responsibility to ensure that you provide the puppy with an environment conducive to developing good traits, including confidence.

Things to adhere to in order to develop confidence in your puppy:

Rush your puppy to the veterinary doctor at any sign of ill health

The point is, there is no way you expect your puppy to develop into a healthy dog that is emotionally balanced if it's going to lie sick every now and then without due attention.

For a puppy to grow to a dog that you are proud to tag along, you need to ensure you seek the services of a vet whenever you sense that something is wrong with the puppy. This is particularly important when it is a newly acquired puppy, whose natural behavior you are yet to grasp. And since at the early stages it's not easy to decipher when the puppy is ill or bored, it's best to play it safe and seek the services of a professional whenever in suspicion.

Make your puppy's crate puppy friendly

This presumes that your crate training is the first your puppy is receiving. So now, make the puppy's crate comfortable for the puppy. If you keep the crate clean and dry, for one, and then you ensure that you never punish the puppy for whatever reason while it's inside its crate, your puppy will always love the crate. It's best that your puppy associates its crate as a favorable place to be.

And don't even feel sorry for having to confine your dog to its crate. Believe you me, dogs, like lions, are den oriented. So, if you make the crate puppy friendly, the puppy will be taking itself back to the crate for some good relaxation without your prompting. To the young dog, the crate will be like a bedroom or some me-space. And it is, in fact, relatively easy to handle a crate trained puppy than one who is not trained.

Facilitate quiet time for your puppy

Sometimes people tend to forget that the young ones of animals are as delicate as the young ones of humans. In the case of puppies, they need long hours of sleep just the same way babies need to have long hours of sleep. So, ensure your puppy has gotten used to remaining alone. The reason this point is being emphasized is that if you get your puppy used to being picked up and given constant attention by members of your family, it is going to feel lonely, and probably insecure, whenever it is on its own. Again, ensure there is some place in the home that is noise free, a place where the puppy can relax and doze off without human interference. It, definitely, needs quality sleep for it to grow in health.

Ensure your puppy receives training

What's the big deal about puppy training? Well, for one, it prepares your puppy in relating well with people. You need to ensure your puppy is well socialized too so that it grows to be well behaved as an adult dog.

According to Dr. Becker, a veterinary doctor, you need to be prepared to invest some good amount of time as well as energy if you are to mold your new puppy into a loveable canine.

And how do you socialize a puppy?

This is a question that resonates with quite a number of

puppy owners. They think that having a puppy around you all the time constitutes socialization. However, there is more than that to socialization of a puppy.

Certainly, keeping your puppy behind the house or in some room in your house is no way to socialize the tiny animal, no matter how many times you visit it at its resting area. In fact, it is not enough socialization even when you have other dogs in the homestead with whom your puppy mingles.

Ok – then what? Well, you need to take your puppy out of the homestead, where it can see and be in close proximity to new people. Your puppy needs exposure to different environments other than your home, and to different settings where it learns that settings can be different yet safe. The important thing here, however, is for you to guard against overstimulation.

It's no good, for instance, taking your puppy from your quiet home environment and directly to a noisy jazz performance; then to a place where you are having a wild party with friends. That can, definitely, be overwhelming to your puppy. As a result, the puppy can become fearful or even withdrawn. You need to be sensitive enough to know when your puppy is getting restless in an environment; and get it out of there fast. Also, it is important how you introduce these changes – doing it gradually and progressive may be the best way to go about it. Actually it's best to ensure that the process of socialization is as normal and as calm as possible for your puppy.

How else can you tell that a puppy is well socialized?

- It handles touching quite well no matter what part of its body someone is touching it

- It is capable of mingling with people and other animals without being unduly aggressive or even shy

- It is capable of visiting new places and being in different situations without suffering anxiety

- It is capable of exploring new environments and discovering things about it

- It is capable of playing with toys and capable of playing some games; and also responding to various stimuli

- It is capable of taking a ride with people without being disruptive

One thing you need to appreciate is that it is very important that you socialize your dog before the age of 14 weeks. And if there's any lateness, it had better not exceed 16 weeks. Ideally, the best time to socialize your puppy is within its first 3mths of age.

During a puppy's three months of age, it is so eager to socialize that any fear it may have had is easily subdued. The puppy is actually more than ready to have new experiences. The first three months of a puppy's age are, therefore, the most ideal for molding the puppy's behavior and building its character. It is also the time to tune the puppy's temperament.

What happens when you don't socialize your puppy?

Don't even think about it. Dog shelters are full of dogs that missed the socialization experience at the right time. As such, they were discarded because they just couldn't fit among other dogs, and they couldn't live in harmony with people.

When you fail to socialize your puppy as necessary, it is likely to develop deviant behavior like aggression. Alternatively, it may turn out to be so shy that it finds it difficult to survive in public; or too timid to stand up for itself.

In short, you can't afford to abdicate your responsibility to socialize your puppy; otherwise you risk it becoming an unmanageable dog; one that nobody wants around them. And there are various interesting ways of socializing your puppy, including enrolling it in puppy classes or even organized play groups; exposing it to new sights and sounds as well as smells; bathing and even grooming it. A well socialized puppy becomes a well mannered, loveable pet that is confident and well balanced.

After acquiring a new pet, what do you do?

Begin By Taking the New Puppy to a Vet

Is that really necessary if the puppy came from a decent home? Well, it doesn't matter where you got your puppy from. You need to go with it for a vet visit the soonest possible. You need to have it examined by a professional who can tell you firsthand what the condition of your puppy is; if the puppy has any special needs you didn't know about; to get a shot if one was due; and generally to create some relationship with a dog specialist whom you can call upon whenever your puppy needs attention.

Where do you get a vet from?

Getting a vet? Well, that one you can get from anywhere, any time. But a good vet? You've got to do some research or get a referral. For one, you need to understand that different vets practice their medicine somewhat differently. Some are strictly traditional, as in, they practice Western medicine as it is by the book; others have a holistic approach to their trade; and sometimes you find those who combine their knowledge of allopathic veterinary medicine with alternative therapies. And we must mention here that no single type of Doctor of Veterinary Medicine (DVM) can be said to be better for your puppy than others as we don't even know your puppy and we don't know your preferences.

For that reason, it is recommended that the search for a puppy goes hand in hand with the search for a suitable DVM. That way you'll have time to seek out a DVM who matches your beliefs and preferences and whom you feel comfortable with. You even need to pay a visit to the clinic you think you could give preference to, just to ensure that what is practically on the ground constitutes a good environment for your puppy. And you need not only to have a tour of the premises, but also evaluate the attitude of the staff. Just like if you were dealing with a baby, you want to entrust your puppy to a team of staff that is friendly and welcoming; a team that would make your puppy feel loved, and not anxious.

Then, of course, there is the issue of fees. Is the vet as well as the facility charging some reasonable figure for the kind of examination your puppy is going to get? It's no good, really, saying that money is no object, without weighing if the fee is commensurate to the services being offered. And there is also the aspect of checking out how competent the staff is. In this world of today that is littered with unscrupulous people, don't rule out the possibility of having quacks in some smart looking facility. Whereas you certainly want your puppy in a clean and organized facility, you also want to be sure that the staff is well trained and the DMV is for real. This background check is worthwhile because at this stage you are seeking a DMV with whom your puppy is going to have a long-term relationship. And you want to entrust your puppy to someone who enjoys serving animals, and not one who is in it just for the money.

When you book the vet's appointment for that first visit with your new puppy, inquire if there is anything you need to bring with you. But just in case you don't get that information in good time, just take it upon yourself to take a quarter sized specimen of your puppy's stool, well packed in a plastic bag. Chances are that the DMV will want to check it for signs of parasites; and if your puppy has any internal parasites, then it can receive the appropriate treatment.

Chapter 4: General Principles in Puppy Training

First of all, why do you want a puppy? Do you want to have a great experience with your puppy? If so, then don't make training a dreaded affair for both you and the puppy – make it fun. In fact, don't begin a training session just because you should, if you are not feeling up to it. If you are feeling bored or stressed, you are surely going to transmit that negative energy to your puppy and the training will be a bore and a bother.

Here are some rules that will guide you in puppy training:

Make puppy training fun

Your scheduled training time should be a time to look forward to; not a reminder that causes you anxiety. To ensure you don't strain your puppy during training, make your training sessions reasonably short – between 5min – 10min is sufficient enough time to teach your puppy something and still keep it motivated.

Here's the catch – reward positive response from your puppy and do not reward non-responsiveness. Of course, in the initial stages of training you can repeat a command or an instruction, but if the dog does not provide the expected response, take a short break.

After a moment, you can resume your training, but this time issue a command that is much simpler than the earlier one. Once your puppy responds appropriately, you can proceed to issue the more complex command you had tried before without success. And hopefully will recall how it goes.

And who will argue with the adage that all's well that ends well? When it comes to puppy training, it helps your endeavors a lot when you end each session on a high note. It actually makes your puppy cherish the just completed experience, and makes it approach the next training session on a positive note.

So, how do you end on a positive note and this is not a kindergarten class where you can end with a fun song?

- Well, back to commands – only this time issue one of the simplest commands; one you are certain your puppy will adhere to.

- After your puppy gets responds appropriately to the command, reward it for the good work

- Now, issue a command that the puppy should understand to mean 'the end'. A good example of a suitable ending command is 'free'; or 'dismiss'; or 'release'.

- Just ensure you are not using a common term as your ending command. If you use a word like 'okay', for instance, don't you think you'll be confusing the puppy, since it will be hearing the term every time, everywhere?

Anyway, you want to end your training session feeling good at what you have just done, and your puppy feeling excited about the whole experience. That's why it matters how you finalize your session.

Familiarize your puppy with the basic commands

If you begin to speak to your puppy in sentences, that will be as good as singing an unfamiliar song to it – pretty much what happens to a baby. If even the size of vocabulary the baby can retain in its mind is limited, what would you expect if you converse in complex sentences? When it comes to training your puppy, you need to pick a select few commands that are relevant to your relationship with your young dog. You can call them obedience commands.

Here are some of the most basic of them:

- Come; sit; stay; heel; stay

- Sit-stay; down-stay; off leash

- Leave it; cease; stop it; enough

If you think about it, when in school, you often found yourself loving the subject you were good at, and not liking the one you performed poorly in. Similarly, when a dog can grasp your commands, it feels motivated to learn from you and respond accordingly. And it often grasps those commands that are simple and direct. Obviously that's the way to go if you want to keep your dog motivated to learn.

And remember the reward system is such that you only reward for correct responses. As such the dog loves the session if it is getting rewarded frequently. Still, on your part, patience is paramount. Remember you'll be teaching your puppy using human language and not dog language; so you to expect your dog to learn your commands like a, b, c, d would be expecting magic.

Do not even contemplate punishment in training

Do you remember the warning given earlier on in the book that if you are not in a good mood you need to skip training? One of the reasons is that it is bad to take it out on your puppy because if you do it'll hate training. The point you need to register is that training sessions should be upbeat; exciting; and relaxing.

However, since you know it is not fun for the sake of it, you ensure you reward every correct response that the puppy shows you. What you should not do under all circumstances is punish the puppy for failing to respond appropriately. Instead, you ignore that response, and you, obviously, don't reward it.

To be clear, you should not execute any punitive measures during puppy training sessions, like:

- Yelling; hitting

- Hanging; chain jerking

- Electric shock

In short, nothing that would introduce negative energy should be introduced in training. In any case, it is well known that a dog feels good to please its owner; so when it responds poorly, it is not out of stubbornness but misunderstanding or inadequate training. In fact, the motivation you give your puppy for appropriate responses – like food; toys; and even attention – is enough to motivate the puppy into doing its utmost to respond to its best ability.

Time your highest reward to coincide with training

The reason you want to reward your puppy the highest during training is that then you motivate it into concentrating in the training and into obeying your commands. After all, training will mean receiving the greatest rewards. And obviously, training a motivated dog is much easier than one whom you have to convince to pay attention.

Effectively, therefore, here is the best way to tailor your reward system:

• Training just before meal time

The best time to hold your puppy training session when the reward you have in mind is food is just before its meal time. At this time, if the puppy does well and you reward it with something to eat, it will value your reward more than anything else you could think off; it will already have begun to think of feeding. And whatever other command you issue after some food reward, your puppy is likely to respond to it fast and with enthusiasm. Why? It will be looking forward to another similar reward – some more food.

- Training when the puppy is longing for attention

Your training is likely to be greatly effective if you hold the session soon after you have come back after many hours; possibly after work. At such a time, your puppy really longs for time with you. So if you enter into training almost as soon as you get home, and then every time your puppy responds appropriately you do some petting or give it some loving attention, it's going to feel great and well appreciated. It's going to feel that the reward of attention you are giving it right at that moment is the best ever. Needless to say, any other command that you issue will be met with readiness to obey and motivation.

- Schedule the exercises according to puppy's energy levels

If you want to train your dog in something like leash down-stay, for the sake of obedience, just precede that with some exercises that will get the energy out of your dog – at least moderately. You don't expect a dog that is steaming with energy to just sit put without getting restless and eager to stand up and expend its bubbling energy. In short, reclining positions as training commands are not good for your early training stages. Wait until your puppy is a little bit tired; and hence glad to rest.

Use your puppy's favorites as rewards

This point is in reference to the food rewards that you give to your puppy when it obeys your given commands. If your puppy loves cheese over and above other foods, opt to use it as reward because then, your puppy will be more than eager to obey your commands in order to enjoy some cheese. And, of course, cheese here is just an example of some foods that puppies could die for. Others love liver that is freeze-fried, and such other niceties.

Remember you are not using this training session as the puppy's mealtime. So you are expected to reward the puppy with just small bits of whatever food you choose each time. Also mind the texture of the food you use as reward. It should be food that is not likely to crumble, because if it does, it's bound to divert the puppy's attention from its training as it tries to gather the crumbs.

And how should praise be?

If you want to reward your puppy by using praise, whatever you say to it, say it in high but pleasant pitch. In fact, let it sound like a singsong. Your puppy will understand that you are happy with it. And don't, of course, forget to portray enthusiasm in your voice.

And what is the best way to pet your puppy?

We are talking of your puppy here and you should, by now,

be able to tell the kind of petting it enjoys. If it enjoys stroking, you surely know it. Incidentally, if you are going to use stroking as a way of telling your puppy congratulations, you were on point in that one, leave the top of its head alone. Most dogs do not think much of your top of the head stroking. Instead, stroke your puppy's hair that is on the side of its face – along the grain manner, so to speak. In short, you are not trying to ruffle the hair but to stroke it smoothly. And in case you are using scratching as a way of petting reward, do that on your pet's chest.

Time your reward properly

You see, a dog is not like a school going child whom you can reason with; maybe say I'm happy with your performance but I won't reward you till tomorrow afternoon when I can visit the shopping mall. If you communicate that way with the child, there'll be no motivation lost. However, the only way a puppy is going to understand that the good deed directly corresponds to its obedience or adherence to your command is by rewarding it instantly. Advice from expert dog trainers is that you reward your puppy within half a second of the puppy responding correctly. That way, it is going to understand that there is a direct connection between its behavior and your nice deed.

Spit out short commands

'Spit' here is used positively. It is the manner of pronouncement that comes across when you use the most suitable commands. It is advisable to use absolutely short commands. Good examples of words that are suitable as puppy training commands include sit; out; down; off; quiet; leave it; and such others. If you check those commands carefully, you'll realize that they all end in consonants.

It is advisable that you use short commands that end with hard consonants as words that end in vowels are bad fits for use as puppy training commands. And one reason for this advice is that dogs usually take 2 min at the longest before they lose sense of what you were saying. Also you are advised not to keep repeating your command – once telling is sufficient. If the dog doesn't respond within reasonable time, consider that a failed command.

Learn to use the exception carefully

There are some instances where the rule of short word for a command is broken, but you need to avoid misusing the leeway you have. The command that can exemplify this exception to the rule of brevity is 'come'. The main reason is that you need to call out the puppy's name first. Then say 'come'. After the puppy responds to your command, you would be expected to say to it, 'Good Boy'. And, in fact, you are even encouraged to address the puppy as 'Good Boy' the instant you call out his name, and possibly even after saying 'come', so that it can understand that you are not calling it to dish out punishment but for good reasons. That way the puppy will not be hesitant to come to you.

Chapter 5: How to Understand Your Puppy As You Teach Obedience

Now, do you whip your dog into steadiness and concentration or what do you do to keep your puppy attentive and obeying your commands? Well, for sure, any form of whipping is a no-no; that's abuse and it isn't acceptable, so brace yourself for some discipline too as you embark on training your puppy. Alright, what's the way out then?

Getting your puppy interested in what you are trying to teach isn't such a big deal when you know the right approach. Here are some basic recommendations:

Keep your training short

Once you keep your training sessions short, your puppy will remain interested in training. You already know what they say about too much of something, right? If you keep your puppy training sessions very long, the poor thing will be bored and lose interest after the minutes begin to drag.

Keep changing your training commands

The point being said here is that you need to have different activities for every training session. You surely can't expect to keep a young one interested, be it a puppy or a child, by engaging it in one activity all the while. Can you imagine teaching your dog the command 'come' from the start of the training session to finish? Even you, personally, might begin to register boredom.

Keep individual activities brief

We are advancing the point of variety to spell out the necessity to allocate only a short time to each activity. In short, it's not just variety that matters, but that each activity takes only a short period. Expert trainers recommend not more than 5min for each activity in a continuous episode. Still, you can return to the activity later, after an interlude during which you could be doing other activities.

Make a game of your training sessions

It's relatively easy to train a puppy when both you and the puppy a having a blast. It is, however, relatively difficult when you make the training session appear like a session of stern preparation on how to invade Mars. So, as much as you can, make the puppy training session fun.

Vary your training environments

Much as you think that familiarity is good, it can sometimes wear down curiosity and enthusiasm. So, instead of confining your puppy training to strictly the living room, just for example, why not use the kitchen sometimes? And if not the kitchen, you still have some hall, or some garden space or some other safe area. In fact, you can also use your daily walks to sneak in some training. It would be fun!

Actually when you train your puppy in different places, there's a plus that comes with it because the puppy gets to master the command, and to know that it is applicable irrespective of the location. It would be disappointing to have your dog master, say, the *stay-down* command within your training area that is your balcony, and then when you issue the same command, say, in public, like outside a shopping mall, the dog stares at you unmoved like it would a hot potato.

Teaching the Puppy Good Table Manners

Oh no... You aren't surely imagining this is fork and spoon business – because it isn't. Teaching your puppy good table manners is about teaching it to remain calm at table whether there is human interference or not. It's about teaching the puppy that just because someone stumbles on its feeding bowl doesn't mean they've suddenly developed an appetite for dog food!

This is how to train your dog at table:

a) Do not succumb to your puppy's every demand, including food. If some food you are holding wasn't meant for the puppy, for the sake of training, do not give it to the puppy even if it expresses desire.

b) Sooner or later your puppy is going to become assertive. And when that time comes, it had better be assertive in a good way. It'd be a disaster to have a dog that aggressively demands to be given what does belong to it. In fact, if a dog establishes such a trend, it can easily become socially unfit.

c) Be keen on your puppy's behavior at mealtimes. It is common for puppies to brace themselves for battle during mealtimes. Train your dog to know that the presence of people around it as it eats does not constitute a threat.

d) Train your puppy to handle interruptions well

It is important for your puppy to understand that people can innocently get in their way, and mostly young children, whose behavior is generally unpredictable. There are a few things you can do to train your puppy to keep cool when distracted at mealtimes. Here are some:

- Every now and then, imitate the behavior of a child. You could, for instance, step on the puppy's feeding bowl when the puppy is busy feeding.

- Do not just disrupt the puppy and leave it at that. Immediately you kick or bump onto that bowl, drop some nice treat for the puppy. That will neutralize any hard feelings it was beginning to develop towards you for hitting its feeding bowl. Its reasoning will be like, Oh, I get it; it doesn't mean that any time someone interferes with my feeding bowl I'm going to be stopped from feeding.

- Reward the puppy for remaining calm at mealtimes

Interfere with anything that will distract the puppy. This means that it's not just the puppy's feeding bowl that you can hit or purport to stumble onto; you can also push the puppy itself, the way a child can inadvertently bump on the puppy. You could, alternatively, roll some toys around the puppy; even when you know quite well that toys are likely to attract the puppy's attention. If it remains calm and does not jump at you or the toys, immediately drop some nice treat into its feeding bowl, and it'll understand that to mean you are happy with its behavior.

e) Address the issue of a growling puppy

It is advisable to do the exercise of interrupting your puppy at mealtimes every so often; and definitely, not always. However, if you notice that instead of your puppy grasping the concept of reward it still remains, kind of aggressive, growling at any sign of disruption, take that as a serious matter.

And if this is serious, how do you move forward with your puppy training? Well, seek the advice of more knowledgeable people, like:

- Some professional veterinary behaviorist

- A dog trainer who is certified

Learn to read your dog's body language

To be a great puppy trainer, you've got to be able to understand a thing or two – and preferably more – about your puppy's body language. Since you don't expect to hear *Mama* or *Papa* from your dog, the best you can do is to learn to read what it means when it physically does this or that move.

A puppy wagging its tail, for example, cannot surely be expressing the same emotions as when it's contorting its face. If you are able to interpret what your puppy means through its body language, you will be in a position to interpret its intentions too. For you to succeed, the movements to monitor are usually those on the puppy's mouth; its ears; its eyes; and, of course, its tail.

Puppy depicting signs of aggression

Of course, you know here we are not talking of its kilos but the way the puppy appears. If you see your puppy trying to stand tall, that time when it has its ears as well as tail sticking out straight, know that your puppy is bracing for some aggression. In most such cases, your puppy will also have its chest pushing out and the hair on its back as well as its neck significantly rising. The puppy here is generally trying to feel bigger than its actual size. And at times the puppy may even be growling and slowly waving its tail.

Dog showing submission

When you have a mature dog making itself appear as small as a puppy, take that as a sign of submission. Ordinarily, if an adult dog is confronted or irritated by a puppy, it kind of tells it off, so to speak, and won't dare attack it. It's good to understand the different dog behavior so that you don't confuse the meaning of various situations.

For a dog showing submission, you will notice it crouching almost to the ground in a sideways manner. And in that time, the dog will be holding its tail low and not wagging it. And if the dog is in a kind of confrontation with another dog, you'll notice the submissive one licking the face of the dominant one. The same case applies when the dog is relating to a person. Something else that will indicate submission on the part of your dog is rolling on its back.

Reading the Tail Language

Do you think the puppy is wagging its tail because it's pleased with you? Well, maybe; maybe not. There are times that your puppy will wag its tail for different reasons. And if you are a puppy trainer, or you just want to train your puppy into becoming a well behaved and balanced dog, you need to be able to read the different motions the puppy makes with its tail. So, be open to practical interpretations of your dog's behavior and not just assume that every incident of tail wagging is indicative of friendliness or even happiness.

First of all, you need to understand that the breed matters. So how one breed deals with its tail when upset may not be the same way another one does in similar circumstances. However, the general indicators are a good aid.

Here they are:

- Puppy holding its tail upwards at an angle of 45°

This one, for sure, tells you that the puppy is alert. In addition, it shows that the puppy is interested in what is happening.

- A slow and stiff tail wagging

When your puppy is slowly waving its tail, in a kind of stiff and not relaxed way, it is clear indication that the puppy is annoyed. You can then tell that the puppy needs to be handled with care lest it manifests aggression.

- Puppy sitting on its tail

The position being described here is one where the puppy sits clamped over its hindquarters. This tells you that your puppy is afraid. That's how dogs that are fearful of something or of the environment stay.

- Puppy with a drooping tail

If you want to know a nervous dog, or one that is anxious, this is it. The puppy's tail is drooping whenever the puppy is afraid, and sometimes it also wags its tail in a stiff manner.

Learn to Read Your Puppy's Eyes

Body language is not restricted to the heavy or main body only, but extends to other physical organs. As such, you should not be surprised to learn that a puppy's eyes can tell you something about its feelings or emotions.

- A dog with eyes half closed

When you see a puppy or even an adult dog with eyes half closed, you can take that as indication that the pet is either happy or is expressing submission.

- Puppy's eyes being wide open

If you see your puppy with its eyes being wide open, you can translate that as a sign that the puppy is ready to do something aggressive.

- Dogs staring at each other

This is very common with dogs that live wild. Any staring down of dogs, and particularly when each is determined not to back down, is indication of a challenge. For that reason, even as you relate with your dog on a day-to-day basis, you need to refrain from staring it down; otherwise it could mistake that for a call to challenge – and you, obviously, aren't ready for a fight with a canine. In fact, if you stare down a dog at a time when it's nervous, it may become outright aggressive towards you as you'll have sent the wrong message; a ready-for-a-fight message.

Learn to read a puppy's smile

Yes, they do smile! But don't mistake a show of teeth for a smile – no; that's danger.

Sign of friendliness

For some breeds, like the Labrador, you know they are giving you a friendly smile when you see this lop sided grin.

Sign of submissiveness

In this case, the same smiley look of friendliness that dogs give you is the same one that you'll see on many dogs, irrespective of their breed, when they are in a submissive mode.

Sign of aggression

Make no mistake – a dog won't show you its teeth to indicate its happiness. By the time you see its lips drawn back and tightly at that, and in a manner that leaves its teeth bare, know there is trouble. It is time to think of ways to appease the animal and not to play around with it.

Sign that the puppy in a mood for play

There are different ways a puppy can show you it wants to play right then. Sometimes you can see it raising its paws and other times just bowing down before you. There are yet other times when you can find the puppy barking; and that's just to draw your attention. Funny enough, you can even find your puppy picking up a puppy or pushing one your way as a way of inviting you to join it in play.

And if you don't seem interested in joining in play and there's another dog around, you may find your puppy trying to provoke it into joining it in play.

Learn to polish your body language

Do you know why it's important to mind your body language as far as puppy training is concerned? It's because body language is the most powerful tool you have to communicate to your dog. It can't comprehend your speech as well as it does your body language. In fact, your puppy is not even as much interested in listening to you as it is to observe you. So, it is important that you develop body signals that are consistent so that you don't confuse your dog. That way, you will be able to tell if your dog is ignoring your instructions or when you are issuing commands understandably unusual commands. And you are, obviously, bound to enjoy each other's company when communication between you is great.

Here are some examples of appropriate body language:

Balancing on a crouching position

When you crouch down before your puppy, and you have your arms well open like you are ready for an embrace, your puppy understands that as a welcoming sign. Keep it that way.

Towering above your puppy

When you tower over your puppy and stare down at it, you are demonstrating power over the poor dog and it translates that to mean that you are a threat.

All in all, understanding your puppy is not rocket science. And remember that a dog learns fast by association. So, whenever your puppy does what is good, what is appropriate, or what you demanded, appreciate it instantly; reward it. It shouldn't take more than one or two seconds for you to reward your dog for something you have liked. This is because you need the dog to always link the reward to its corresponding action. That way, it is bound to repeat that positive action again and again. We mentioned it earlier on that puppies like it when they are rewarded. And so they had better understand what you are rewarding them for every time.

Chapter 6: Learning About Puppy Crate Training

Do you want to have a confident dog? If you want to have a confident puppy, that grows to be a confident dog, there is no way you are going to ignore crate training. Don't pay attention to the quacks of dog care who would like you to believe that a crate is unfit for a puppy – it isn't.

Do you realize that dogs are in the category of animals you can term den dwellers? And you know that a den is a small confinement. That's the kind of place you would find the dog resting if you were to let it out into the wild. It's for the same reason you often find your puppy or even your big dog lying comfortably under some table or chair; or such other relatively small enclosure. In fact, when you are preparing to welcome a new puppy to your home, it is advisable to prepare a crate for it in advance, so that it can immediately mark its ideal resting place.

Are there other reasons you want a crate for your puppy?

Yes, there are plenty of reasons besides making it comfortable. Here are some of them:

- Crate training drastically reduces, if not entirely eliminating, chances of your puppy destroying your house property, including furniture, which dogs often love to chew.

- It also keeps the puppy safe from potentially dangerous material lying around, for example, electrical cables; poisonous liquids and solids; and so on.

- A crate also serves as a great mobile dog house for the indoors; making it easy for the puppy to be relocated from one room to another whenever there is need for that.

- The puppy crate is also great for moving about with the dog when in travel, whether your journey is by road or by air – it is a suitable travel cabin.

- The puppy crate also comes in handy when you are residing in a hotel that accepts dogs, because such hotels usually demand that you have a puppy crate. The reason they usually make this demand is because they don't want your puppy playing with hotel stuff and ruining it in the process. Often when puppies are not in crates, they end up causing damage to furniture, rugs and other material in the room.

Note

- o In case you put a puppy in a good crate and it escapes, it is a sign that the puppy might have had a bad experience when inside a crate; something that makes the puppy associate a crate with, maybe punishment, or such other bad experience. And in that case, you'd have to help the puppy reprogram its mind by possibly rewarding it while in the crate.

- o Dog experts recommend that you provide your dog with a crate all through, no matter its age – even after you are through with crate training and the dog is all grown up. You can even remove the crate door when you don't find it necessary any more, for those kennel crates that allow for door removal.

- o Then you can place the crate at a place of your choice, even under the table in the living room. The most important thing is to ensure that the kennel crate is useful where it is and is not obtrusive.

How to make the crate experience good for the puppy

Did we just mention that a dog is den oriented? Well, what a better way to please one than to make its crate look like a den? One way you can make the puppy's crate get closer to a den is by covering one half of it – the back half – with a blanket. You can also use any other fabric other than a blanket to cover that half, because the end result is essentially to make the crate somewhat dark; just like a den. If you do that well, which is an easy thing to achieve, you'll find your puppy gravitating towards that crate.

One big advantage with providing your puppy with an appealing crate is that it will want to remain there a lot of its resting time. This, as has already been pointed out, is because of the nature of its instincts as relates to a den. Now, again, since the animal loves the place it considers its own, it isn't going to soil it if it can avoid it. So you'll find it waiting until you come to let it out to relieve itself. However, for the puppy to have this kind of discipline, you need to have provided it with good potty training, which in this regard, would include coming for the puppy and taking it outside to relieve itself; making regular potty trips – almost predictable by the puppy in timing.

Point to keep in mind:

For the sake of effective crate training, do not, under any circumstances, force your puppy to get into its crate or to leave it.

Getting into and out of the crate needs to be a voluntary affair. If you make it a point of forcing the puppy into its crate, there is no doubt that your actions will make the puppy averse to the crate. At the same time, if you get used to forcefully driving the puppy out of its crate, the puppy will begin to lose its sense of security. Yet one of the reasons you have a puppy crate is to provide it with a place it can consider private and secure.

Let everything about the crate be positive

And even as we say that the crate should be associated with things that are positive, it is important that this is not just the way you look at it, but that the positive outlook is also from the puppy's point of view. A great way of making your puppy view its crate in positive light is putting treats in it. You can also place chew toys in there or even dental bones.

Also even when you have ascertained that the crate training you have provided your puppy is sufficient, you need to continue making the crate enticing by constantly putting treats in there. You can also make a point of placing toys in that crate, or anything else safe that your puppy values. The whole idea with making the crate a likeable place is to have your puppy entering its crate of its own accord, and leaving it voluntarily as well; or at least when you ask that it does.

Chapter 7: Any Foreseeable Crate Training Problems...?

Let's remember something that was mentioned in some earlier chapter about crates. A dog doesn't require a crate only during its tender age – no. A kennel crate is useful at all times, irrespective of the dog's age. It is actually quite versatile as exemplified by its use during long distance travel.

And in any case, the minute you discard a kennel crate that a puppy has been using, the minute the puppy identifies another secluded place to make its den. That place could be under your dining table, inside your closet, or anywhere else. So, why bother to remove the crate when clearly the dog needs it?

Let's summarize the benefits that come with the use of crates:

- Being den-like, kennel crates provide the puppy with a place it feels secure and comfortable.

- A crate becomes the puppy's own space; just like a teenager's room where the teenager feels good getting away from the rest of the nosy family.

- A crate serves as a safe carriage for your puppy as well as becoming a convenience in dog friendly hotels

- Crates are great for anxious dogs who often suffer borderline separation anxiety.

Other such dogs have a phobia for thunderstorms. The kennel crate then serves as the puppy's safe haven. And it particularly comes in handy when the puppy owner is away from the place the puppy is. In fact, it's always advisable to keep your puppy kennel crate door ajar in case the puppy needs to jump in and regain its sense of security.

All in all, you need to make the crate what it is supposed to be – a place that the puppy loves. Failure to do that can easily result into the puppy loathing the crate, even as it grows into a mature dog. Yet you have seen the many benefits that come with the crate. What are we essentially saying here? We are saying that you need to know the likely mistakes associated with the use of crates and do your best to avoid them.

Here are some of those crate related mistakes:

- Forcefully putting the puppy in the kennel crate

- Putting a puppy into a crate that is uncomfortable, possibly being too small for the puppy's size.

- Leaving the crate bare and boring – with no blankets to make the environment puppy friendly; no toys to play with; and even no treats to make the puppy feel welcome.

- Keeping the puppy confined in its crate for extensive periods on a single stretch. Or even leaving it for a duration reaching a whole 24 hours. Not only does the puppy get too tired staying in the one spot for too long, there is the likelihood of it urinating and defecating right inside the crate. Now, how can such a defiled place be attractive any more, even to a dog?

- Making the puppy's crate the time-out location; that is making it the place for meting punishment.

Such mistakes, as we have seen, only serve to make the puppies aversive to crates. And you don't want that to happen when you have seen how valuable kennel crates are. If you know that your puppy is averse to crates, just observe how much complaining it does when you show it the crate or once it is inside. You'll clearly see that the puppy is not willing to be in that crate. Mark you the rebellion that the puppy makes in a bid to show you its aversion to crates or to practically try and make a run for it, could end up injuring it.

Here are clear signs that your puppy is averse to kennel crates:

- The puppy manifests aggressive behavior, like nipping as well as biting anyone trying to shove it into the kennel crate

- It also protests in form of barking after you close the kennel door after it. You can also see it scratching frantically in an effort to escape, futile as its efforts are.

- The puppy aggressively bites the door of the kennel crate in anger

- For passive dogs, signs of being averse to crates are manifested differently. Sometimes they internalize their negative emotions and end up diverting those emotions in other ways, like:

  o The puppy licking its body, or even licking the inside of its kennel crate

  o The puppy revolving in tiny circles as far as the space in the crate allows o The puppy beginning to feed on its excreta

The lesson here is that as a puppy owner, you need to avoid anything that can make a puppy despise anything to do with kennel crates. You need to handle crate training appropriately. And that appropriate handling of crate training includes acclimatizing the puppy to its crate in a suitable manner; and avoiding anything that is negative to the puppy's emotions, like punishing it within the crate.

Chapter 8: Crate Handling Tips

If you have noticed so far, puppy training is a two-way experience. If you train your puppy well and behave well towards the puppy, your puppy is going to reciprocate. However, if you train your puppy well but then forget to keep your part of the bargain once the puppy has learnt the dos and don'ts, your earlier achievements will be eroded and the puppy is likely to behave like it was absent during some days when you taught the rest of the class. Oh – yours was a class of one... but you get the point, anyway.

The long and short of it is that you need to keep treating your puppy the same way you treated it during training. If you kept a feeding schedule during crate training, continue with it even after the crate training period is over and you'll be comfortable with your puppy's behavior.

Here are other things you need to remember:

Using the collar appropriately

It is important that you remove the dog collar when you take your puppy back to its crate for safety reasons. Unless you want to retain the identity collar, which by its very make should be entirely safe – kind of break-way – there is no reason why you should leave your puppy with its collar on. In any case, there is no training going to take place within the crate and so the puppy doesn't require a training collar therein.

Keep puppies comfortable according to the weather

This warning particularly targets the hot or warm weather, when leaving puppies enclosed in crates could leave them thirsty and uncomfortable. Dog experts would like you to pay particular attention to short-muzzled puppies – those that include the pugs; the pekes; the bulldogs and others. They would also like you to pay special attention to the Arctic dogs; those that are normally thick coated; and they are exemplified by the Malamutes; the Huskies; the Akitas; Newfoundlands and such others.

You need to place some cold water in the puppy's crate because at some point the puppy is bound to get thirsty. You are also advised not to leave a puppy without a minder on the terrace; on the roof; or even inside a car; when the weather is warm. And when it comes to the usual exercises outdoors, you need to keep the sessions short, even when they are just walks.

Don't use a crate that's too large

If you want your trained puppy to hold its poop or pee till you come to set it free, ensure the crate the puppy is using isn't too spacious. You see, when there's a lot of space around the puppy, it is easy for the puppy to imagine that it's fine to move to some corner and relieve itself. But a crate just big enough for the puppy and minimal movement is a constant reminder that the crate is a resting place and not a multi-purpose zone.

However, some puppy owner who has seen a puppy poop in a properly sized crate might think that the writer of this chapter is short on information. That's not at all the case. It's a fact that sometimes a puppy ends up relieving itself inside the crate even when the crate is the ideal size, but there are extenuating reasons for it.

Here are some reasons that cause a puppy to relieve itself in its crate:

- Being too young to have bladder and bowel control

- Consuming a diet that is too rich or too rich

- Consuming extra large meal portions

- The puppy being confined to the crate before relieving itself

- The puppy's gut being infested with worms

- The puppy having loose stool or being gaseous

- Having consumed plenty of water just before being crated

- The puppy having a history of relieving itself in odd confined places in the period before undergoing crate training.

- The puppy being unwell; possibly with a bladder infection; a problem with its prostate; or something just as inconveniencing.

- The puppy being in a state of anxiety, possibly from drastic separation

The concern for many a puppy owner is how to treat the puppy after finding out it has messed up its crate. Can you take measures to discipline it? Quick and firm answer is no, you can't. Just keep your cool, clean the crate and embark on finding out the reason why the puppy behaved in the manner it did. And from there you will know the way forward.

And while we are at the business of crate cleaning, let us

mention that you are advised to avoid using cleaning products that are ammonia based. Reason...? Well, ammonia, if you remember your days as an aspiring scientist in a High School lab, smells like urine. And such smell can only serve to stimulate the puppy's bladder while the puppy is in the crate. Luckily, there are other odor neutralizers in the market, designed purposely for use in areas where pets live.

What's the best duration to leave a puppy crated?

Good question, well answered below:

- For puppies between 9wks and 10wks of age: Roughly ½hr to 1hr

- For puppies between 11wks and 14wks of age: Roughly 1hr to 3hrs

- For puppies between 15wks and 16wks of age: Roughly 3hrs to 4hrs

- For puppies between 17wks and over: Roughly 4hrs to 5hrs (6hrs maximum)

Night time notwithstanding, you are advised not to leave any dog crate for a duration exceeding 5hrs; and if you do, 6hrs should be the ultimate stretch.

Chapter 9: Easy Steps to Potty Train Your Puppy

How easy do you think it is to potty train your puppy? If you can imagine that potty training a child is not itself a smooth ride, you can imagine how tricky it is to train an animal, whose method of communication is nothing like that of humans. If truth be told, it can sometimes be frustrating. In any case, most people want the puppy getting sufficient house training like yesterday so that life in the home can be normal.

So there is, evidently, the element of human impatience to deal with. Sometimes you think the puppy is being stubborn or is simply a dunderhead when, in fact, you are the one whose jumping the gun in the training process or entirely skipping some crucial steps. For that reason, everyone purporting to train a puppy needs to acquire the basic information, or to have basic guidelines, so as to avoid frustration in the process of potty training your puppy.

In fact, the need to learn basic potty training cannot be overstated when you take into account the fact that different puppies often present unique challenges as individuals. Still, your instincts have a significant role to play in the whole potty training process. The most important thing in all of this is to foster a relationship of trust between you and the puppy you are training. The puppy needs to feel your love for it if it is to sail with you.

So, the big question is: Is potty training doable?

And the simple answer is: Why not? If there is no way out, then you've got to do what you've got to do. Otherwise, can you imagine having a puppy that soils your seat cushions, spaces under your tables, and anywhere and everywhere? That cannot be tolerated and it isn't even bearable even if you wanted to ignore it.

Unfortunately, training a puppy can be tricky, particularly in its early days. This is because a young one eats adlib and seems to burn up energy much faster than the bigger dogs. That therefore means that the need to excrete is more frequent for puppies than for mature dogs. In fact, eating more frequently is not the only reason these young ones tend to do the excretion thing more often. At that tender age, the puppies are yet to develop bowel control or even bladder control. So you can't expect them to hold their stuff for long.

So, what is to be done by any puppy owner who wants a dog

that behaves with decorum as far as relieving itself is concerned? Well, this is where potty training comes in. But before that can be effected, your puppy has got to understand the business of being in its homestead; its den. And that means that any area that the puppy considers its resting place is not to be soiled. Yet again, knowing its den and being able to control its bowels and bladder are two different things. For that reason, when the puppy is still tender, you need to avail yourself very often so that you can direct it to the right place to relieve itself. In short, it is your diligence that is being called upon here to ensure that your puppy gets on the right track as far as house training goes.

And if you want to know what to expect in the long run, well, brace yourself to potty train your puppy until it gets to the age of 6mths. The puppy may have gotten better with potty training over the weeks and months, but they don't really become efficient until they are half a year old. In fact, some breeds take even longer than that. So, any errors on the part of the puppy that you may witness when it is four or so months should not discourage you. Just stay the course and your puppy will outgrow this messy business. And hey! Don't try to figure out why the puppy is failing sometimes, because really, there often isn't any good explanation for it. However, you need to adhere to some basic potty training guidelines and you'll be fine.

Here are the fundamental potty training guidelines:

- Allow the puppy to access its toilet area on a frequent basis. That way, it is likely to be prompted to relieve itself even if it hadn't initially registered pressure.

- Whenever your puppy pees or defecates at the place you have established as the toilet area, make a point of rewarding it. That motivates it to repeat the behavior; it longs to be rewarded and that's normal.

- Never punish your puppy for the error of relieving itself outside the designated area. Punishment doesn't give you the results you'd like to see. Instead, you breed new unfavorable behavior.

- Avoid feeding your puppy as if it's living wild. In this regard, the standing rule is that you need to adhere to a particular feeding schedule. That way, the puppy will often feel the urge to relieve itself at more or less the same time every day.

- Maintain a diary

The kind of diary we are referring to here is one where you write down the time when your puppy relieves itself. And you are expected to know this because you'll be monitoring it regularly, to notice even the times when it inadvertently pees in the wrong place. The diary will help you adjust the times you visit the puppy to help it move to its toilet spot.

Any idea how often a puppy needs to potty?

What does it matter how often the puppy feels pressed? Oh, it does matter a lot. Having the information on how regularly your puppy needs to potty would make your work a lot easier, because then you'd just set an alarm to alert you when you need to go and take the puppy out for the taxi service; that is, ferrying it from its crate to its designated toilet area. But no – things are not that easy in potty training these young ones.

There are a lot of unknowns in the peeing and pooping schedule of a puppy. Sometimes its timing will depend on when the puppy ate or drank last; how much physical activity the puppy has had; its personal conditioning; and other factors that even the puppy owner cannot put his or her finger on. So, you are left with no choice but to be vigilant the same way a nursing mother is. Let's say, your only savior in this affair is sleep. Puppies love their sleep and you won't normally find them relieving themselves when asleep; so for that duration they are in wonderland, you are saved the hustle of babysitting, so to speak.

However, it's good to have a timeframe to work with. And the timeframe here is half an hour to forty-five minutes. That's the average time a puppy normally takes between potty sessions – just 30 – 45 minutes. You can't risk being away longer than that; otherwise the puppy might mess in its crate or wherever else it is when the urge comes. And that doesn't help your potty training efforts.

You need to be committed

Oh yes – that's no news, really. But then, much more committed than providing regular taxi service to the puppy? Yes! If you and your puppy have set loose boundaries so that the puppy can roam the premises as it wishes, then it's up to you to follow the puppy around. If it drinks something along the way, note that down; if it chews a bone, that's your business to note; if it does some exercises like running in circles, it's also for you to note it down.

Studying your puppy's behavior in its run up to pooping or peeing is your business. So, if you feel that it's a hustle to be where your puppy is all the time, do the most logical thing – confine your puppy to its crate or some kind of pen. It's the only way you are going to minimize, if not eliminate, potty training errors.

Make Puppy Feeding Regular

What's the big deal with feeding times if there's no shortage of dog food at home? Well, that's the reasoning good old grandmas used to have concerning kids. Now kids, too, are trained to feed according to preferred schedules – and it's not for reasons of food rationing or something that dire. It's for health reasons and other disciplinary reasons like we are trying to inculcate in puppies.

Here's the main principle: If you feed your puppy regularly, it will need to do the eliminating thing regularly too. So, essentially, your taxi service trips work pretty well at regular intervals. And how easy that makes your life! Of course, not to mention that it reduces chances of your puppy making potty mistakes.

What you need to do, in addition to feeding your puppy at regular intervals, is to monitor how the puppy responds to such a schedule. Some puppies have the need to poop after half an hour, while others delay up to one hour after feeding, before they feel the urge to relieve themselves. It is upon you, therefore, as the puppy trainer, to establish what routine your puppy has. It will help you to know how to program your taxi service trips.

Please Don't Be Careless

Some people are known to be careless (or is carefree more polite?) and they want to avoid making scheduled puppy feeding trips. So what they do is put plenty of food at the puppy's disposal and the puppy can feed, sleep, get up and feed again, and so on. That's the kind of feeding that experts of old used to recommend for beef cows – because theirs was a fattening mission. They called it feeding adlib. Here, it's all wrong; feeding your puppy without measure.

Here it is, actually, in black and white:

- Make your feeding random and the shitting will be just as random. You can't expect any better. Is it not true that you reap what you sow?

- Expose your puppy to food all day long, and it will cease to view food as something valuable. And with that notion, food ceases to be helpful to you as a reward in training. In fact, the puppy stops associating you with provision of food because the food is there before the puppy all the times. That is not good for your entire puppy training program.

Chapter 10: Mistakes to Avoid In Puppy Potty Training

Does it mean everything is smooth for life when you train your puppy in matters of the potty? Of course, potty training gets you a well behaved puppy and one that makes for good company, but it doesn't guarantee you that mistakes will not happen. Even when it comes to human beings, mistakes do sometimes happen because of varying circumstances, but such unpleasant happenings are just temporal.

When it comes to puppies at their tender age, they are just like babies. They are not capable of controlling their bladder so that they can hold back urine until a certain hour or until conditions are right. They are also not capable of controlling their bowel reflexes and that's the reason they relieve themselves without due consideration for the location or timing. It is for this reason that earlier chapters have spoken of the taxi service, where you program yourself to go pick up the puppy and take it to its designated toilet area before it can soil its crate.

And, of course, the need for patience in potty training such young puppies has already been mentioned. In addition to being patient, you also need to be firm and consistent in your potty training. And as long as you are being fair, your response to the puppy's behavior, which entails only rewarding good behavior, is bound to pay dividend. As regards potty related accidents, adult dogs too have them occasionally; but most of the time you can identify a good reason for that if you care to find out. At times it's because the pet is either on diuretics or even on steroids. The good part, however, is that the dog resumes its discipline once it's through with medication.

It is also important to note that there are certain dog breeds that are more difficult to potty train than others. Of particular note are the small breeds. And once you have this information, you can psyche yourself to be extra patient in house training when you are handling the naturally difficult ones.

Beware as you buy your puppy

Here you are not being discouraged from adopting a puppy or from buying one from places that have them for disposal, but you need to know what to expect of your puppy, so that you can, in turn, prepare to handle it appropriately.

This book mentions that puppy training needs to begin early.

Well, that doesn't usually happen to puppies that are held in big numbers in a small area. So practically speaking, expect to get an untrained puppy when you acquire your puppy or even an adult dog from a pet store; a flea market; some unrefined backyard breeder; and such other places. Such animals are often confined inside cages for most of the time, so there's no way training for them is feasible.

In short, you'll be taking with you a puppy that eliminates waste in the same place you put it, simply because it has not been trained in any other way. If you acquire a dog from a shelter, you are likely to face a similar problem because the dog has been confined inside a kennel for so long that it has developed a new norm even when it had been earlier potty trained.

Behavior that can exacerbate potty training issues

The negative behavior that this chapter seeks to highlight is actually your responsibility; your shortcoming. It is good that you know what some people sometimes do and end up sabotaging their own training efforts. In fact, when you are well versed in matters of training or dog handling, you'll notice some things that dog owners do which are bound to affect a dog's behavior negatively.

Haphazard feeding

Have you noticed that some puppy owners treat them the way grandmas of old used to treat their grandkids? Sheer spoiling, it used to be. The puppy barks, the owner throws it some food. It jumps and clings onto him or her, and the owner reaches out for some bites to give it. And then when you think the puppy is likely to be hungry you serve it some food, this time in its bowl. When will you ever know how much the puppy ate and when? Can you really tell? Right! If you can't tell the puppy's feeding time or even the amount you fed it, it's only logical that you shouldn't be able to tell when that puppy is going to poop. That's why you find your puppy has pooped in its enclosure when you least expected it, or it has pooped in some place nobody can expect if you let it out free.

But in all fairness to the puppy, can you say the puppy lacks in potty discipline when you do not follow any feeding schedule? If you don't want to sabotage your potty training efforts, serve your puppy the food amount that you usually give it, and then leave the puppy feeding. Come back after some duration of between 10min and 15min and take away any remains.

A tendency to be inconsistent

How do your bowels behave when you feed on a balanced diet and how do they behave when you feed on refined foods? How do you find your bowel movement when you do exercises in the course of the day as opposed to days when you sit all day long? How do your bowels and bladder behave when you feed several times in bits as opposed to days when you have normal regular meals? You can be sure that the body behaves differently in different circumstances.

In the same vein, you can expect your puppy to feel the urge to relieve itself at odd times when you feed it without a plan or a schedule. Days when you walk your dog, its bowels are bound to behave differently from when you skip taking out for a walk. And it's not that your puppy also enjoys this feeling of peeing and pooping at odd times. Instead, that unpredictability deprives the puppy of its sense of security; and it doesn't feel good on the overall.

The advice you need to take away here is that it is important to keep to a regular feeding schedule as well as a regular potty schedule. That way, your puppy will learn to hold its pee or its poop until you show up to release it, because it will learn over time that its anticipation is not in vain.

Failure to understand your puppy's language

It's funny how some puppy owners expect their puppies to understand them, while they themselves make no effort to understand their puppies. How can two beings work together in harmony if communication is not effective? If you can't tell when your puppy is saying I'm pressed I want to go relieve myself, you are failing. And that's the kind of failure that gets the puppies peeing or pooping anywhere.

Are you worried that you can't understand the language of barking? Well, that's funny because you really don't need to understand it. Your puppy communicates in different other ways, and as we mentioned earlier in the book, puppies usually communicate using their body language. And if you recall well, dog experts encourage you to communicate to the puppy using more of body language than speech.

Here are signs that your puppy needs to relieve itself:

- The puppy puts its head down

- It begins to sniff the ground or floor around it

- It walks around nervously

- Usually the puppy walks in circles

- The puppy looks anxious

- It starts whimpering or barking

- It paces up, down and all around

Untreated infections

If you expect that one day your puppy will bark something that comes close to *vet* or *med*, you are lost. Yet there are times when your puppy needs the services of a veterinary doctor and its body requires medication. It is your duty to ensure your puppy visits a vet for routine medical check-ups, and also when it begins to behave out of character, like relieving itself where it's not supposed to.

There are many occasions when a puppy's potty schedule gets disorganized because of Urinary Tract Infections, commonly known as UTIs; and other times because of parasites.

Causing your puppy confusion

Taking the example of human beings, if I were to ask you to accompany me somewhere, and then I lead you to a shop where I buy an item, and from there I knock on a friend's door and say hello, would you really be able to tell which of the two actions was the main mission and which one was a by-the-way? I'd surely have to tell you that clearly. This is how confusing it is for puppies, when you take them out on a potty mission, and then you proceed to engage in play soon after that. If you had just let the puppy out of its crate, it will not be sure as you return it if you had come for it to play and relieving itself was a by-the-way, or you had come for it on a potty mission and the playing was a by-the-way.

So, to avoid confusion:

- Set a particular spot for potty purposes

- Ensure potty time is strictly that – potty time and not playing time

When you let the puppy do exactly what you released it to do, there is no risk of confusion on the part of the puppy. And soon you'll realize that every time you release it at the scheduled time, it will make its way directly to the potty spot. The puppy even gets to associate the smell from the potty area with peeing or pooping even when you make a point of regularly clearing the place. And that smell is very useful in stimulating the puppy's bowel and bladder reflexes.

Chapter 11: Training Tracking To a Puppy

How hard do you think puppy tracking training could be? In actual fact, it's nothing like potty training. Unless you have a propensity to be boring, tracking training will be fun. For one, tracking is not something you are going to introduce to your puppy – it's been doing it since birth. Yes; tracking calls for use of the sense of smell, and a dog does it naturally as a matter of fact.

Do you know that a puppy doesn't open its eyes immediately after birth? Well, how do you think it locates where its mother is when it wants to suckle? And if you will well recall, in its early days, the puppy's brain isn't even working. The truth is it's that natural sense of smell that helps the puppy track its mother. So you can see clearly that what you are being called upon to do in puppy training is just streamlining your puppy's tracking prowess. And if there is fun to be had, it is in training a puppy in tracking.

Anyway, easy as it is, what is the best system to use?

Identify an appropriate training venue

You can't plan for an activity before you have secured a venue, can you? That's how it is, too, with track training. You want to have a place that is conducive for training, where the goal of your puppy training can be achieved without undue inconveniences.

It is important to point out from the onset that you have the liberty to train either indoors or outdoors when it comes to track training. However, in the initial stages of training you had better be indoors with your puppy. The reason is simple. Remember that tracking has a lot to do with following a scent. Now, if you introduce some scent outdoors, don't you think there is a high chance the intensity of that scent will be reduced courtesy of natural elements like wind and temperature?

And there's something else you need to take care of as you select your ideal training area – the prevalence of distractions. You cannot afford to train your puppy in tracking amidst distractions, be they from other dogs, from people moving about, or even from loud noises. The puppy needs to be in an environment where it can focus and process what it is picking with ease.

Pick a suitable object to be tracked

It is good to go with what has been tried and succeeded; and in the case of track training, expert trainers have observed that a puppy enjoys tracking down its favorite toy. The puppy has a strong sense of how its toy smells like, and picking up its scent is not very difficult. If you pick on a particular toy to use for track training, keep to it the whole training time. Consistency helps in puppy training.

Still, using your puppy's favorite toy is not a hard and fast rule; rather, it is a suggestion. You can, by all means, use another object that you deem fit for puppy track training.

Begin by playing fetch

Anyone you know ever woke up one morning and ran a marathon without rehearsal? Very unlikely, indeed... In puppy track training, you don't just delve into the track training session without some warm up. And the right warm up is one that kind of introduces the essence of identifying something – and that is the game of 'fetch'.

Not only will the game of 'fetch' get the dog in the mood for training, but it will also set the its mind towards the issue of looking for something. However, don't sap out the entire puppy's energy in warming up. It is recommended that you spend between 10min and 15min playing with your puppy, before you engage in track training.

Teach your puppy the stay command

If your puppy already knows the stay command, otherwise referred to as the sit command, well and good. If not, this is the time to teach the command to the puppy. Here you may be wondering how relevant this could be in track training, and it sure isn't directly linked to it. However, by teaching your puppy the sit command, which means you are telling it to be still and not move, you are essentially training it to be patient.

And if you never thought about it that way, patience is an essential ingredient in learning – yes, in learning tracking too. Experts recommend that you attach the puppy's leash to its collar during that time it is settled in one spot.

Place your puppy's toy on some surface

The idea here is to place your puppy's toy in a location where your puppy can easily trace it; in plain view, more like it. Then initiate the tracking process. Of course, your puppy will easily track down its toy and be very pleased about it. In any case, a dog has naturally a strong sense of smell and it can't be difficult for it to trace something whose scent it has registered over time. All the same, though it isn't yet time to give your puppy a medal, isn't this one instance motivating to the puppy? And you know motivation is necessary if you are to succeed in puppy training.

Put the toy some place as puppy watches

Let's say you aren't pretending to hind anything here. But you'll still be in the process of track training. Is your puppy seated? Well, it can either be seated when you initiate this step, or it could be standing – just not in motion. As your puppy watches you, take its toy and place it at some spot right in front of him, where you are very sure he can see it. Are you wondering what end this could achieve?

Here:

- Get hold of your puppy's leash as it sits or stands wherever it is

- Issue a command to the puppy to go retrieve the toy you just placed somewhere

- Don't instruct your puppy like you are telling a story. At the risk of reinstating the obvious, let's mention here that your puppy cannot decipher long phrases and sentences. So only use the very common verbal cues, and those include:

- o Search

- o Seek

- o Find it

Curiosity now: How does this work out? Does your toy make a dash for its toy? Here is what you can expect:

- You may be lucky to have your puppy get it at the first prompting.

- Alternatively, your puppy may not get it right away, which means it may just yawn or stare at you or into space

- If you notice your puppy hasn't understood your command, assist it to understand by leading it by its leash up to where its toy is lying.

- Let it pick its toy using its mouth

- Now lead your puppy back the same way you came, still with its toy in its mouth, until you reach the spot where the dog was seated or standing initially.

- Once you have arrived back, issue a command to your puppy to drop the toy it is holding in its mouth. At this juncture, you are hoping it has dawned on the puppy that you have just helped it accomplish what you wanted it to do in the first place.

Repeat this exercises severally; placing the toy in plain view and instructing your puppy to go fetch it. After a while, your puppy will register those commands that you are associating with retrieving an item. And you'll have succeeded in that part of puppy track training.

Remember, every time your puppy adheres to your command and fetches the toy, you must reward it with praise and also with something tangible like some piece of dry food that it loves.

Next, stash the puppy's toy in a hidden location

By now, it is safe to believe that your toy understands the commands that mean *search*. So:

- Command your puppy to sit down or just stay

- Let it sniff the toy you are holding just to remind itself of the scent

- Now move away and hide the toy out of sight. Some of the places you could hide the toy you want searched is under a chair, a table or some other furniture; or even some place beneath a cardboard box.

- Return to where the puppy is; and issue one of the search command

What you want to find out is if the puppy will be able to trace its toy without having seen where you hid it. If it does, it should, definitely, know that you need the toy brought back to you.

This stage of puppy track training is different from the earlier one because your puppy now is being called upon to use its sense of smell and not just its sight. As we mentioned earlier on, a dog is normally born with a strong sense of smell. However, during a track training session, you are trying to get the puppy to direct its sense towards a particular item. Once your puppy succeeds in bringing back the toy you just hid, reward it instantly. And you should remember to reward it for every mission it accomplishes well, no matter how many times you send it.

Hasten the tracking by using wind

If there is a way you can get the wind to blow the scent of the item the puppy is searching for towards the puppy, it means the puppy will be able to detect the scent from afar and move in that direction. This is how you do it:

- Hide the toy some place

- Then move upwards where the wind is likely to hit your face, and stand there with your puppy

- Now issue the search instructions to your puppy

The wind will be coming towards you and the puppy, and the wind will be carrying the scent from the toy towards you and the puppy will detect that.

Obviously, this intensity of scent and the fact that it is reaching your puppy's nose even before it nears the toy makes it much easier and much faster for the puppy to trace the hidden toy.

Use a helper to hide the puppy's toy

This time you want to take the track training further, and

have someone else help you to hide the toy. This means that as the puppy goes to search for the toy, there is nothing else familiar you can attribute to its success other than the toy's scent.

- Issue the stay command to your puppy

- Stand beside the puppy in a way that it can see you are keeping it company

- Let the person assisting you in this training stage take the toy and hide it someplace where you and the puppy cannot see from where you are stationed. Notice that the puppy actually saw the person picking up the toy and going with it; and the only thing your puppy doesn't know is the new toy location.

- Stay put until the person who went to hide the toy returns

- Now issue a search command to your toy and watch it move to go track the toy.

At this stage when you are making the puppy's toy search more challenging, let the person assisting you hide the toy in a place that is easy to locate. Since the puppy was used to you doing the hiding, having someone else do it is a bit challenging for the puppy; it may give the puppy mixed feelings. Remember the puppy is used to your scent and not the other person's scent, and it is used to trusting you and not the other person. That's why it's good to keep the toy location relatively easy to find.

Once the puppy gets the hang of it, the person can begin to pick the toy as the puppy watches, and going to hide it in a place that is not obvious; a place harder to locate. The idea is to escalate the difficulty of the search as the puppy gets comfortable with the tracking. You don't want to increase the difficulty in a sudden manner because you want to ensure that the puppy remains motivated. Getting things wrong is, obviously, disappointing, even for the puppy, and the puppy can easily get demoralized and lose the will to engage in the search.

If you want to ascertain that your puppy has learnt tracking to an admirable degree, let the person assisting you move away towards one direction while holding the toy, leave the toy somewhere out of sight, and come back to where you are from another direction. In fact, you could even be doing something in the meantime to make the puppy pay attention to you rather than to the person assisting you. That person can now go back, pick the toy, and do the actual hiding of the toy; burying it where it is difficult for the puppy to find.

By now, the person has mixed up the directions in the puppy's mind, and in addition, the toy has been hidden in a place where it is very difficult for the puppy to locate it. When the person returns to where you are with the puppy, send the puppy to search for the toy. If it succeeds this time, with all the complexity of the search, consider your puppy track training successfully done.

Chapter 12: Mistakes to Avoid In Puppy Training

Do you know there are some mistakes you could make when you are training your puppy only to realize, in retrospect, how silly they were? Like issuing a command to your puppy three or four times as if you imagine your puppy has a problem with its eardrums... Surely, when your puppy doesn't adhere to your instructions, it's a matter of comprehension and not hearing.

Anyway, some of these things we take for granted sometimes prove to be tricky just because we are human; and what we call common sense sometimes proves to be not so common, after all. Bob Bailey, a famous dog trainer, says that the art of puppy training is quite simple. The problem...? Yes – he says that simple as dog training is, you can't say it's easy. What? How paradoxical can it be, simple but not easy? Well, he says that when it comes to applying the principles of dog training, it proves very difficult for many people. Hence, his stand that training is quite simple, but at the same time it is not easy.

Still, when you know the common errors that puppy trainers are prone to, you can make a conscious effort to avoid them.

Here are some of the most common puppy training errors:

Re-enforcing bad behavior

Look – how do you bring yourself to summon your puppy for some cheese pieces after finding it jumping on your couch? What message are you sending to it? Aha! Very likely, you never gave much thought to it, but the minute you bless your puppy with cheese or some niceties the puppy loves, you are essentially telling the puppy: Well done – what you have just been doing is marvelous and as your minder, I'm showing my gratitude by giving you something you cherish.

There! The next minute or hour, or even the following day, your puppy will be there jumping on your couch again. You have been re-enforcing bad behavior. And that is why the puppy may just look at you and continue jumping on the couch even when you issue commands like *stop* or *cease*. Even frowning or contorting your face as you command your puppy to stop the bad behavior may not be effective. The reward system is the most effective, and you have been abusing it.

For another example, suppose you want your puppy to

remain indoors until a certain time when you personally take it for a walk or let it out to play. If you are indoors with your puppy, you expect the puppy to remain inside when you open the outside door because it's not yet walk time. However, it may be jumpy and try to push against your legs in a bid to dash outside. You need to halt and issue the stop command or the return command. However, if you develop the attitude of, *Oh, this puppy is too jumpy; ok, go out if that's what you want,* you have created trouble for yourself. Giving in to a puppy's whims is not the way to help in training.

In instances like this one where the puppy dashes to the door when it sees signs of you leaving, and then you actually allow it to go out when you open the door, that is re-enforcing bad door manners. You need, instead, to train your puppy in polite door or exit manners, and reward it every time it behaves appropriately. If you command the puppy *back inside* and it adheres, give it some delicious bites. As we have already seen, dogs value food and when you give some food token, it re-enforces its behavior.

The practice of lumping

Lumping is a big mistake. Is it really? Anyway, what is lumping, in the first place? Well, lumping means trying to teach everything in one session. For effective training, you need to break down the training so that you have simple small steps, where you pick each of the steps for training every session. It is very confusing, for example, to try to train a puppy in obeying the command of lying on a mat, by sending it to the mat when you are standing next to the mat; then sending it to the mat when you are standing about two feet away from the mat; followed by a command to the puppy to go lie on the mat when you are standing in some corner of the room. The puppy may obey your command in the first instance and the second one, but by the third time it's likely to halt and look at you in wonder and a degree of uncertainty. Is this human friend of mine sure of what he wants? That's very likely what your puppy will be thinking by this time.

The lesson here is that it is best to begin with baby steps whenever you want to train your puppy in any one thing, and let the puppy feel comfortable with that particular thing, before you can decide to graduate the training to a more complex command or even to vary the manner of issuing the same command.

The tendency to generalize commands

If you train your puppy to obey the command, *sit*, when both of you are in the kitchen, do not assume it's obvious the puppy will heed the command when you are out in the playground. Experts say that dogs are very discriminating when it comes to commands. Maybe they are inclined to be exact and specific. So, if you have trained your puppy to obey certain commands when indoors, train it also how to adhere to the commands when outside the house if you think you are going to use them there. Try out the commands in different environments if you think the commands are going to be useful in varying environments.

Dogs usually register your physical manifestations and also the environment with more seriousness than they do your verbal language. And maybe that is just as good because someone trying to issue a command to your puppy, for instance, to relieve itself somewhere at your balcony will be disappointed even if they use the same verbal command that you use. This is because as you took your puppy through potty training, the puppy made a mental note of how its potty area looks like. As such, it's not going to mess up your compound just because a mischievous person tells it to. So, remember, puppies usually ignore generalizations.

Failure to understand your puppy's emotions

Successful training cannot surely be one-way traffic. It is not for your puppy to watch and read your body language effectively; you also need to watch your puppy and read its body language, as well as noises as accurately as possible.

Unless you have taken time to watch and understand how your puppy behaves when it's feeling unwell, when it's feeling uneasy with the environment; when it's having a bad vibe about someone; you cannot possibly enhance your training, and you cannot possibly build a helpful relationship between you and the puppy.

Your ability to read your puppy's behavior will, for instance, let you know when your puppy is uncomfortable with an area; whether it's because of the noise within, the presence of other dogs or something just as unsettling. However, if you understand your puppy well and you can see there are factors that are causing it stress, you'll postpone any training you intended for that moment. It's not viable to try training a puppy when it is feeling stressed. The best you can possibly do is work on making the puppy comfortable. If you succeed in making the puppy feel at ease, you can then proceed with your intended training.

Failure to understand your puppy's communication

Surely, if you train your puppy so often to read your gestures, your moves, your body language, and even your human voice, why wouldn't you deem it necessary when your puppy produces a certain noise – possibly at a certain level; with a particular sharpness; and so on? If you issue a command to your puppy, do you get it when it responds in a particular manner, other than what you instructed? If your puppy touches you in a particular way when holding its tail in a certain way, have you any idea what message it's trying to pass to you?

It is important for you to understand your puppy's responses and other forms of communication so that you know how to proceed in responding to it in turn. Once you and your puppy understand each other's way of communicating, training becomes relatively much easier.

Overusing verbal commands

Don't bother your puppy with unnecessary verbal instructions or repetitions and imagine you are doing anything progressive as far as training is concerned. That's in fact only a way of convincing yourself that you are serious with your training and enthusiastic as well, but it doesn't really advance your puppy training. So, cut the self deception that dogs do understand human language – your puppy doesn't understand yours, much as it may seem to listen to you with interest.

Instead, zip up your eager lips and use your body language – and even luring, if need be – to teach commands to your puppy. Not issuing verbal commands does not jeopardize your puppy training. You can combine your verbal commands with your body language later, after your puppy has learnt to associate certain commands with certain gestures of yours.

Being mean with your re-enforcements

Do you remember when you were in High School and you kept getting questions from a certain topic wrong, exam after exam? How did you feel about that topic in due course? Very likely, you tackled such questions only when you had no choice; and it's not surprising if you didn't want to be close to people who were discussing the topic. That's the kind of feeling that dogs have when they can't get your instructions right again and again. It's obviously frustrating.

And guess what makes it even more frustrating for a puppy in training? Well, there is no reward for a failed task! And you know how much dogs like treats. As we have learnt in earlier chapters, you need to reward your puppy with something that it loves, mostly foodstuff, every time it obeys your command and does it correctly. You actually give your dog a treat within a second or two of fulfilling the command as a way of affirming to the dog that what it has done is good – call it re-enforcement. Now, if your re-enforcements are few and far between, or if there is entirely no re-enforcement, your puppy will begin to show lack of interest in your commands. Oh – oh... Anything you think you can do about that? Nothing! Your best bet in keeping your puppy in class, so to speak, is ensuring that your instructions are simple and straightforward. And before you issue a new command, issue a familiar one first. That way, your puppy responds well to your command, and you get a legitimate reason to reward it. The more your puppy gets commands right, the more you reward it. So you find yourself with a high rate of re-enforcement – just what you need to keep your puppy interested in training.

Chapter 13: For Puppies, First Show First Learnt

Have you realized what a mess some people make by trying to train in what they themselves have not learnt? What content are you going to provide and what techniques are you going to show your puppy if you have learnt none? Without a doubt, you are going to use your imagination. And if truth be told, some people's imagination is too fertile for comfort. You may, for instance, watch as someone instructs a puppy to sit down, but what you observe is just funny, if not ridiculous.

Sit. Nothing doing... *Sit!* That's a shout now; but nothing doing. *Sit down!* And a big push on the puppy's butt as the person shouts at the puppy. Then the misplaced pride: Yes... I told you my puppy understands me when I issue the sit command. No! The puppy doesn't understand your sit command! You just pushed its butt and the puppy, inevitably, found itself in a sitting position. That's precisely what happened, you quack... You didn't succeed in commanding your puppy! You've just used force on your puppy and got your way. That's bad training, and your puppy is going to stick with it and present a massive problem to its new owner.

If you are privy to the proper puppy training techniques, you'll be watching this quack training in amusement. A puppy that has received this form of crude training can never be on the same wavelength with a dog owner who has been handling well trained puppies. Having read the preceding chapters of this book, you already know that no force should be exerted on a puppy in the name of training. Moreover, a puppy like the one you've just witnessed will never sit down before it feels some massive force exerted on its butt. And undoing any such bad behavior taught to a puppy becomes an uphill task for the new puppy owner, as puppies learn very well what they are taught first. That's why it is best to train your puppy well from the very beginning.

In this chapter, you are going to learn the most common forms of bad behavior that puppy owners teach their puppies without realizing it. And, of course, once you have learnt them, you are going to avoid doing them yourself.

Here is some mess that dog breeders inadvertently make while training:

Covering the whole pen or puppy crate with newspapers or shavings; pee pads; wire and such material

If the puppy's private resting place looks all uniform, how

can it be expected to distinguish the potty spot from the rest of the space? You need to train your puppy well, and particularly be keen within the puppy's first 3wks. You need to be regular with your taxi trips and in the process train your puppy to hold its urine in anticipation for the taxi trip. It's the same way it does once you train it well; suppressing the urge to poop until you come to take it out to the potty area.

Reneging on your promise

Is there really a promise you can make with a dog? Well, you don't have to say anything, but actions, truly, speak louder than words. And it's not just in puppy training, incidentally. It's there in commercial law as well. If you are used to sending your assistant to collect goods from a store on credit and then you pay later, the day that assistant of yours decides to play crook and collect goods without your instructions, then disappears with them for personal use, you will be liable to pay for those goods as well. The point is, by your conduct, you have made the store owner believe that your assistant conducts business on your behalf; and you are, thus, prepared to pay any goods that the assistant collects.

As far as puppy training goes, you are used to rewarding your puppy with food bites whenever it obeys you. For example, when you call the puppy, it comes to you expecting something edible from you, no matter how tiny. If you start calling the puppy when you want to cut its toe nails, when you want to give it a wash, and so on, the puppy is going to get pissed off. It's going to wonder: I thought our agreement is that every time I obey and come to you there's supposed to be something for me to munch. What's happening that you are not keeping your side of the bargain?

If you continue like this, sooner or later the puppy is going to begin ignoring your call command. And it's you who'll have confused the poor puppy. Food is motivating and so the puppy comes because you've already taught it that there's a reward after an act of obedience. If you are now wondering what you are supposed to do when you want to groom your puppy or something like that without confusing it, it's easy.

- Just go and pick up the puppy – don't call it. However, just so you know, the puppy doesn't become this sensitive until it has reached the age of 5wks. Before that, you can summon the puppy for anything and it won't make a big deal of it.

- Alternatively, call the puppy even if you want to trim its toenails. But once it has responded to your call, reward it instantly with something to eat; then proceed with your toenail trimming.

Training by default

Surely don't you find it necessary to schedule a puppy training session instead of hopping into training without a plan? Now, there are those times that you actually end up training your puppy, but if someone were to ask you what you taught that day, you wouldn't have an idea at all. That is because you just behaved in a certain way without intending to make an impact on your puppy, but your actions and behavior ended up teaching your puppy something. Unfortunately, often in such cases, you'll have taught your puppy bad behavior.

A good example is when you confine your puppy into a whelping box that has solid walls for too long. What happens then when such a puppy gets restless because it can't even see what's going on outside its enclosure? Since it has no way of getting out of that whelping box, and it does not know how else to behave in such circumstances, it ends up jumping up and down as it barks. Possibly it hopes it might be able to see outside if it jumps high enough. That is what is known as default behavior – the way a puppy, or even an adult dog, behaves when it doesn't know any better.

And guess what? Nuisance barking and noisy jumping was the least on your mind when you put your puppy in the whelping box. So you are likely to dash to check out what is happening. And chances are that you are going to pick up the puppy and give it some welcome petting; and it will be pleased with you. What do you think you have just accomplished by your response? Easy: you have just re-enforced your puppy's behavior of jumping in the whelping box and barking. As such, do not expect that behavior to stop any time soon. By your actions, you have trained your puppy badly.

Rooting randomly on the ground

Do you call sniffing all over the ground and eating whatever the puppy finds natural? Well, it will be second nature to your dog if you don't train it well at the right time as a puppy. Your role is to train your young puppy how to track scents so that it grows to be a great and reliable scenting dog. And, of course, you need to introduce your puppy to scents in its very early weeks; begin to train it in scent trails when it's around 5wks of age; and then train it in more complex tracking, including trailing as well as wood walks after that.

Now, do you know what happens when you don't make a deliberate effort to carry out crate training, track training, and such other necessary training when the puppy is still young? Well, the puppy begins to root for food randomly around the grounds where it happens to be standing at any one time. And, of course, the reason for rooting on the ground is so that it can chew on whatever it finds and eat it. Do you know if what the puppy finds is digestible? Do you know if it's healthy or poisonous? The thing is, without you taking initiative to train your puppy, it will develop behavior that is both dangerous and unbecoming. That behavior can be extreme so that:

- Your puppy lands on a veterinary surgeon's table, having swallowed hard items that are a threat to its health

- You cannot walk the puppy on a leash and enjoy the walk because it keeps rooting on the ground for whatever treats it can find whether it's hungry or not. And sometimes it keeps dragging you where you didn't intend to go, just in its wild search for treats.

- Training the puppy right later in life becomes a daunting task for you or whoever else might adopt the puppy. Whoever tries to train such a puppy in obedience; search and rescue; and such other skills finds it an uphill task that takes a lot more time and patience than it does training a puppy with fine behavior. Remember, as experts say, puppies learn best whatever it is that they learn first.

So, ensure you train your puppy properly at the right age before it begins to develop unwelcome behavior. And as you train your puppy, take care of this:

- That you place the its treats right on the track

- That the puppy you are training is not exposed to a situation where it has to compete with other puppies during training

- Refrain from dropping the puppy's treats on the ground. Instead, hand the treats decently to the puppy. This behavior has various advantages including training your puppy to receive treats from someone's hand without inadvertently biting them.

The reason for this order is that undue competition for treats leads to development of chaotic as well as random behavior as opposed to the tracking you are supposed to be tracking. Despite all the literature being presented to you, do not be overwhelmed by the thought of training a puppy from scratch. It is something you and anyone else can do when they have learnt the simple skills such as those presented here. But above all, the reason it's so easy to train a puppy right from its early age is that it is the time puppies are primed to acquire skills; to learn. Therefore, you'll not need to push yourself too hard. In fact, you'll find yourself enjoying the experience.

Chapter 14: How To Tell Your Puppy Calls For Training

Are you a professional dog trainer? No...? Well, many dog owners aren't. In fact, a good number of them are not even amateur dog trainers, because they don't even bother to train their own puppies. You may be surprised at the number of people who think that dogs learn by default and that is as is expected. As a result, you get to mix with people who may imagine you are looking down upon them just because you are avoiding their company when in a group. Yet the problem is not them but the behavior their dog manifests.

Whereas some puppies and adult dogs are simply a nuisance, others are outright dangerous. They bite at the least provocation. The shameful thing is that these dogs do not necessarily bite because that is their inherent behavior; they often bite because they are either untrained or poorly trained, or not socialized or poorly socialized. As a result, they end up mistaking innocent contact with people for threat. If you can't train your puppy at the right time, why not, at least, enroll it formally in an obedience class?

This suggestion is not to be taken lightly because, really, modifying a dog's bad behavior so that the dog becomes acceptable in society is not the easiest thing. You and your puppy can easily become pariahs in your community or within your circle of friends just because nobody can stand your puppy's behavior. Who wants to have a deviant puppy around, anyway, that keeps barking at will? And when it comes to the risk of biting, is that some unpredictability anyone wants to joke with? They better miss your company than be exposed to your ill-mannered puppy.

Horrifying Statistics Of Dog Injuries

Have you heard them say that numbers don't lie? Well, they surely don't. And that's why people feel confident making decisions based on research that is based on actual figures and not imagination or guesswork. Listen to what experts say about dog related injuries and even deaths:

- In the US, about 1,000 people are treated in the *Emergency Room* (ER) with injuries caused by dogs each passing day. If that's not a scary number for a 24hr period, I don't know what is.

- In the period between 1982 and 2014, research conducted in both the US and Canada showed that the breeds most accused of causing human injury and, sadly, death, were the pit bulls; the mastiffs; the Rottweiler; as well as the boxers.

- Some small size breeds are also guilty of causing disfigurement to people and even death. Research done by the *American Veterinary Medical Foundation* reported that Jack Russell terriers rate somewhere at the top when it comes to dog breeds that implicate serious injuries to people by biting.

- Chihuahuas were also rated among the top five breeds that were reported to bite people in a research that covered the period between 2012 and 2013, within Denver. Pit bulls were also rated high on the list in this regard.

Any lesson from the statistics – or is it good enough to feel learned?

Well, one undeniable lesson is that you are likely to be moving about with a ticking time bomb when you have a puppy that is entirely untrained and one that is not socialized. And that means, your puppy could cause havoc at the least provocation and do something fatal that could land you in jail, or cause you to be hit with an extremely painful fine.

Number two, you are learning that size is not a determinant when it comes to the danger of an untrained dog. A tiny untrained dog can be just as dangerous as a huge untrained dog; and definitely, more dangerous than a big trained dog.

We can also aptly declare, following the example of *The Humane Society* that enrolling your puppy for training does not necessarily make your puppy an angel in animal form, so to speak, but at least, it drastically reduces the risk of bad and, thankfully, dangerous behavior.

If you have just acquired a new puppy or a new dog, can you tell if it's dangerous or badly behaved? Yes, you can. You associate with your dog or puppy everyday and you can see how it reacts to human interaction. It surely is not like having a kid in boarding school where you only get to notice some bad behavior over the holidays. However, just in case you aren't sure if to tolerate some behavior from your puppy or enroll it right away for obedience training, here are some telltale signs of looming danger:

Aggressive behavior

Are you thinking how obvious this should be to a dog owner? Well, a good number ignore it when they see their pet growling at another for no good reason. They also ignore it when they notice their puppy barking at a passerby. The medical director of *Brixton Pet Health,* who is known as Dr. Steve Chen, puts aggression as one of the top indicators that your puppy needs urgent and serious training. And even when your puppy is only showing aggressiveness in matters relating to food, and particularly aggression directed at kids, that's something to be addressed fast.

Having a penchant for barking

So are you to consider barking serious because it interferes with your conversations and your relaxation? Well, barking does that alright and it's annoying, but it is not the only reason you want your puppy trained. The more important reason is that this tendency to bark, and sometimes lunging at people, is indicative of an underlying issue of a behavioral nature. And only an expert can tell you exactly what underlying problem is, and help you address it properly.

The tendency for puppy to chase its tail

Do you think this is funny? Actually some people literally stop to have fun watching a dog chasing its tail. But guess what? That's a sign that your puppy is not emotionally healthy; beginning with being bored, to whatever else only an expert may be able to identify. A canine behavioral expert by the name of Dianna M. Young says that when a puppy is prone to this behavior of chasing its tail, it shows that it is under-stimulated.

The tendency to jump at people

Just because a dog owner hurries to quell any fears and assures you that all is fine when the puppy jumps on you on entry to the home doesn't really make you feel good about the whole experience. Anyway, who wants a strange puppy's paws sprawling all over him or her when they may not even have a puppy at home themselves; or when they have a tame puppy at home? Evidently, your puppy needs the services of a professional trainer if it can't welcome or greet a person without clinging onto them.

A tendency to ignore a first call

Don't underrate bad manners like ignoring your call when you make it the first time. If you had trained your puppy to understand a call and it passed the training, and now when you summon it you are left wondering why it is you can't get the response you expect, it is best to seek professional attention.

Tendency to pull on the leash

Why do you walk your puppy on a leash? Obviously – because you want to lead it where you want. But is that what always happens with all dog walkers? No! Sometimes you notice someone literally being pulled by his or her puppy even with the leash well held. Other times you find the puppy trying to run in different directions when still in your hold. That is surely not good behavior, much as it may trigger some laughter from people watching.

As Dr. Chen says, if it is increasingly becoming necessary for you to wrap the leash around your own hand, and that is for the reason of keeping your puppy under control, that there is real trouble; and a sign that the puppy needs professional attention.

Chapter 15: Embracing Apparent Puppy Dominance

Have you observed a dog behaving in a certain manner and thought to yourself, this man (or woman) must really be controlled by this dog? For instance, a person may be heading for his bed but his dog precedes him there. First of all, the idea that a dog should lead you as you two take a walk is seen by some people as a sign that the dog is dominating you. In fact many people are so afraid of being dominated by their dog that they won't even eat with the dog at table. They view acts like the dog sleeping on your bed as dog dominance. However, there is great news for you if you've been afraid of letting your puppy have it good – treating your puppy gently does not lead to dog dominance. That belief is a myth.

Instead, if you want your puppy to obey you, and not just do it but do it consistently, try influencing it gently. Many puppies that obey their owners' commands on first issuing have been gently influenced and not coerced into submission. Likewise, you can allow your puppy to feel good sharing your bed and yet have the same puppy enter its crate when you so desire. You can allow it to lead the way when you are walking about yet have it stop when you want; and without much fuss. In short, you can create mutual understanding between you and your puppy, where the puppy does what it enjoys doing and obeying your directions when you issue them. The important thing is for you to be sensitive to the likes and dislikes of your puppy, as you set house living rules for it. That way, you'll not have to fret over the possibility of your puppy ever taking over your home.

Debunking Puppy Domination Myths And Gently Influencing Puppy

Barking

People who are anxious about the possibility of being dominated by their puppy often translate the puppy's barking to mean that the puppy is claiming to be in charge and in control of your relationship. However, there are myriad reasons a puppy can bark. Did you even know that a puppy can bark just because it's bored? And sometimes it barks out of fear or even anxiety.

How can you gently alter your puppy's barking behavior?

Train your puppy to bark and then stop

That way, it will learn to express its emotions, whatever they are, and not make the barking a nuisance.

Engage the puppy in exercise

What has exercise to do with cutting the barking? Well, we mentioned boredom as one reason a puppy barks. Why then not stop the puppy from the barking mode by engaging it in exercise. You can appreciate that from a human perspective too. Can you really speak of boredom after you have completed a game of tennis, a rope skipping session, or such other fun exercise? So, introduce your lovely puppy to members of your household, so that even when you are not around the puppy can still engage with them in play. You can also acquire some appropriate toys for the puppy.

Stop being an enabler if you are one

This point relates to the behavior of attending to the puppy every time it barks. What happens when you attend to the puppy because it has barked? Well, it understands that to mean, man, when you want attention, just bark. Such behavior on your part has the same effect as that of spoiling a child in a negative way. Even refrain from yelling at the puppy in an attempt to make it stop barking – even yelling, irrespective of how stern you look as you do it – ends up re-enforcing the nuisance barking behavior over a span of time.

However, if you observe that the puppy's barking is incessant despite your efforts at making the puppy comfortable, the best option is to take it to a vet. That way, it can be checked for any medical condition that may be causing it to bark in an unexplained manner. It is also important for you to try and establish what it is that makes your puppy anxious, in case you notice it has unfounded fears. Then try and work on desensitizing your puppy to those triggers.

Urinating in your house

Some people believe that the reason your puppy urinates in the house is to make it known to you that you are in its tuff – marking territory. But that surely isn't correct. Just like barking, there are different reasons why a puppy may not relieve itself where you expect it to – its toilet area. One of the reasons could be as simple as urinary tract infection. Another one is the dog being unneutered. It has been observed that fixed dogs rarely pee in the house. And then again, your puppy may just be ill-trained. By the way when we speak of neutered dogs we are referring to dogs that have been castrated and if they are females we are referring to those whose reproductive organs have been surgically and entirely removed; and for females the term *spaying* is preferred as opposed to neutering.

In effect, therefore, it may be pretty difficult to pinpoint the reason your puppy is urinating inside the house; unless, of course, you have an obvious reason, like the puppy having come directly from a shelter. So, to be able to tell what the underlying issue is and hence address it accordingly, why not just consult a vet? Then if the puppy is medically fit, go back home and embark on house training afresh. You also need to re-evaluate the way you handle your puppy and see if the way you treat it has something to do with it peeing in the wrong place. Do you, for instance, avail yourself to let your puppy out to its designated toilet area? During training, do you reward your puppy appropriately to make it appreciate fully when it is that is considered good as far as toilet manners are concerned?

Assuming the dog dashes into the kitchen to try and eat before you

The truth is, your puppy doesn't care if you eat before or after it as long as it can have a go at a meal in sight. Aren't these animals scavengers, anyway? So, your puppy being drawn to food is nothing strange. Debunk the myth, therefore that your puppy jumping onto kitchen counters is a show of domination. Number two – your puppy may not even be interested in food at the time it's jumping onto kitchen counters. It may just be bored. So do what you need to do to ensure that your puppy isn't dying of boredom. You can often tell when your puppy is bored because it won't just be obsessed with kitchen counters – you'll find it trying to dig into the trash bin, often causing a mess.

The question is: How do you go about curbing this problem of the puppy jumping onto kitchen counters or on your dining table? The first one is training. Every time your puppy jumps on a kitchen counter, command it to get down; and once it obeys, reward it immediately with some nicety.

You may also get your puppy the kind of toys that you can stuff with foodstuff because then those toys will attract the puppy even more – they are aptly described as interactive toys. And in the process of animatedly playing with the toys the puppy will burn its excess energy and not be tempted to jump onto tables and counters. Can you also see that you'll be solving the problem of puppy boredom?

Assuming puppy jumps onto you to assert themselves

It's surprising how humans can make a big deal out of nothing. If a kid can raise itself and wish to cling to you when it has missed you, why would you think it strange that a puppy would wish to do the same? You and the puppy have a friendly bond and sometimes it just wants to hug you and say hi. Other times it's just fun to do some jumping and you happen to be great support for the puppy. And, of course, there are those instances you happen to own a puppy whose previous owner had inadvertently conditioned it badly – call it bad training if you will. Now, how can such behavior be avoided?

Well, it's all doable when it comes to puppy training. Embark on training the puppy to sit down whenever a visitor enters the house; and every time it does that you ensure you reward it with some delicious treat. Also ensure that you only reward your puppy when it's on its all fours – even if you were to reward it but then you realize its forelegs are raised, withdraw your attempt to reward. Your puppy will make a connection between raising its legs and lack of a treat; while noting the link between having a treat and being on all fours.

Ensure too that the other people interacting with your puppy are not re-enforcing the puppy's behavior of jumping onto people. Tell them clearly that if ever the puppy jumps on them they should discourage it by give it their back.

Dogs pulling on the leash to assert domination

Do you agree sometimes human beings are unduly concerned when it comes to puppy behavior? Think about a puppy pulling on the leash and the owner getting worried of puppy domination; yet the puppy is simply excited about the prospects of an outing! Who doesn't enjoy the fresh air and natural scents the outdoors provides?

And there are those puppies that will pull on the leash only because they are used to it and they've not been discouraged before. So it's up to you to let the puppy know that the behavior of pulling on the leash is not acceptable. Here we are saying, do a bit of re-training and consistently refuse to allow the puppy to pull on its leash while you are taking a walk. Keep encouraging the puppy to remain close to you and reward it for that behavior when you are training it. Experts recommend that you teach the puppy the *heel* command. On the contrary, if it is pulling on the leash when you are beginning the walk, refuse to proceed with that session in a way that the puppy can relate the retreat to its pulling.

Dog pushing against you to enter a doorway before you

A puppy hastening to pass you in order to enter a place before you is not necessarily indication of the puppy trying to dominate you. Sometimes puppies do that just to satisfy their curiosity – they want to see what it is that lies therein. How then can you conclude that the behavior is a bid to dominate you when really you just happen to be in the puppy's way?

Still it can be unsettling, you might argue; and yes, that may be so; but the puppy may not have been taught otherwise. Why not take it upon yourself to train the puppy to always wait till you have entered the doorway for it to follow? This calls for you to train the puppy to understand the *stay* or *wait* command. If you successfully do this, your puppy will be giving way to you so that you precede it while entering any door and lead the way when leaving any enclosed area. Baby gates can also help you in training the stay, wait or even sit command with reference to doorways. And in the meantime those baby gates serve to deter your puppy from moving uncontrollably from one area of the house to another. At the end of your training, your puppy will have learnt that wherever there is a doorway, you are the one to lead the way, either getting into or out of a place.

Puppy refusing to heed your come command because of the boss attitude

Have you tried to find out if your puppy has been trained in the come, stay, sit and such other basic commands? You may be assuming wrongly that your puppy is bossy towards you, while in reality there is no effective communication between the two of you. A puppy will only come when you call when he understands your instructions. There are also instances where a puppy has been trained, but commensurate treats lack whenever the puppy obeys – lacking of re-enforcements. What makes instant treats helpful is that the puppy understands your *come* command to mean the puppy should adhere now, that is, instantly, and not at leisure.

There are other times too when even a properly trained puppy can fail to heed your *come* command. A good number of those instances your puppy is actually distracted by company; either fellow puppies or people around. Even trees, cars and such other fluttering or moving objects can distract the puppy so that your command attracts little attention from the puppy. As you can see, therefore, you need not jump to conclusions that either your puppy has become stubborn or is trying to lord over you.

To alleviate this problem of your puppy being indifferent to your come command, you need to re-train it in the come *command*, but this time you do when the puppy is still on its leash. If you do a good job of reinforcing your puppy whenever it obeys you, before long it will be heeding your command on first hearing. But your reinforcing should be such that there is no doubt in the puppy's mind how happy you are with its behavior. You also need to warn against punishing your puppy for not adhering to your instructions or commands. If you begin punishing your puppy because it delayed in obeying your command, soon it's going to associate coming to you with punishment.

Your puppy mounting others or even you to exercise dominance

Your puppy is just playing; stop reading too much into it. Sometimes it could also be trying to relieve stress. Luckily, this is playfulness that you can replace by issuing a command that is totally different, like *sit, stay* or even *down*. Of course, you need to reward any positive response from your puppy because that is what will reinforce the behavior of, say, sitting, whenever the puppy feels the urge to mount another puppy or even a person.

Dogs climbing onto furniture to show they have authority over them

This is as mythical as can be. How do you feel when you sit on a cushioned seat? Comfortable... - right? Your puppy, too, knows what comfort is about and it loves it. So, it just gets onto the seat to enjoy the same comfort as you do; you need not worry about domination or the act being an attempt at asserting authority.

If you still don't like having your puppy sharing your seat with you, train it to appreciate the *off* command so that if you find the puppy on the seat when you want to sit there, you can instruct it to get off and it instantly adheres. In case there is no time you feel comfortable your puppy resting on your seats, whether you are there or not, make use of baby gates or even tethers, to ensure the puppy's movement towards the seats is restricted.

The other thing is that since you already know the puppy cherishes comfort, it is important that you provide a comfortable bed for it to lie on. If you manage to do this, every time you find the puppy lying there, ensure you reinforce the preferable behavior by giving the puppy a treat.

The long and short of it is this: If the only reason you wanted to keep your puppy off the seat is fear of it dominating you, shed that and embrace your puppy's company. Sharing a resting area, whether it's your most valued couch or just an ordinary sofa, with your puppy doesn't change the form of your relationship as long as all other basic rules remain enforced.

Note

There are people out there who consider themselves dog trainers, and this may be true for most of them. However, there is a difference between someone who has the information and skills from way back in the day, and one whose knowledge and skills are regularly updated according to fresh scientific findings. The Association of Professional Dog Trainers is always updated on what dog training methods work well and which ones are counter-productive. Do appropriate due diligence whenever you want to engage a puppy trainer, so that you are sure you are engaging someone who has already changed his attitude and perspective as per new scientific findings.

You don't, for instance, want to engage someone who whips your puppy whenever it fails to follow an order in training; or one who tries to intimidate it in various ways. In fact, before you let someone else train your puppy, it is best that you have a discussion about the methodologies the person intends to use on your puppy. If they tally with what you know to be appropriate, well and good, otherwise, you may consider skipping the person's services till you can find one with whom you agree. After all, as the puppy owner, you'll be expected to reinforce the training your puppy receives from the trainer every time after the formal training.

Chapter 16: Basics Of Housekeeping

How much do you remember about the housetraining explained in previous chapters of this book? There is plenty of it that we shall summarize in this chapter, in a way that you can recap in just a few minutes.

First of all, let's remember that housetraining involves training your puppy to poop and pee in a specific spot, and restraining it from relieving itself anywhere away from that chosen spot. Is it alright to punish the puppy when it relieves itself in the wrong place? Well, straight answer is no. If you go the route of punishment, very likely your puppy will not learn anything new that you intend to teach it. Instead, it will take it that relieving itself indoors or in areas that you haven't indicated is a dangerous undertaking. Note – it is dangerous; not that it is wrong.

And if your puppy takes it that danger looms only when you are around, it may avoid messing when you are around but do it when you are away. On the contrary, when your puppy learns what is right and what is wrong, it will do the right thing whether you are in the vicinity or not. In short, training is preventive and better than punishment in effectiveness.

Make a point of rewarding your puppy

You need to reward every good behavior from your puppy; otherwise how will it know the difference between obeying and disobeying or ignoring commands? Besides, rewarding your puppy motivates it to do what it has learnt to be right and preferable.

Here are some of the simplest, yet very important, rules of housetraining:

Keep your eyes on your puppy regularly+

Of course the reason for this rule is so that you know where the puppy is at any particular time, and control its actions accordingly until it is fully house trained.

Offer treats to the puppy as necessary

Where housetraining is concerned, you need to reward your puppy whenever it relieves itself in its designated spot

Ensure the puppy does not relieve itself in any area of the house besides the designated toilet area.

How do you do that? Easy – since you are keeping tabs on your puppy's whereabouts, you are bound to notice when it's doing what it's not supposed to. If for instance, you find the puppy relieving itself in the wrong place, go ahead and interrupt it in a gentle manner, and then redirect it where it's supposed to be.

And how do you then re-train it so that it uses its designated toilet area and that alone for peeing or pooping? See below:

Spare at least one hour to put your puppy on a leash and then go out with it. Lead it to its potty and then stand right there as you wait for it to do some pee or poop business. Be patient because this waiting period could lag up to five full minutes. When the puppy finally pees or poops, put on that happy face as you reward it with some delicious treat. Believe you me; a puppy rewarded is likely to repeat the particular behavior over and over again.

Chapter 17: Handling Puppies and Kids Together

Can you safely have puppies and kids in the same environment?

You can indeed! That is, as long as you can train each of them how to behave towards the other. And as you train them, you need to take into consideration the value of having a harmonious home.

Going by the teachings of earlier chapters, you can see how important it is to be patient in training puppies. The same case applies to training kids. You need to be prepared to invest time training and monitoring them. Once trained, puppies and kids often enjoy a wonderful time together.

How to help children and puppies live in harmony

Keep them supervised

The reason these two – kids and puppies – need to be closely monitored is because the children, particularly the very young ones, may engage in rough play, without realizing that they are playing with an animal, incapable of reasoning. They may also stumble onto the puppy accidentally and upset it, and you can never tell how the puppy is going to react in such situations. It may begin to growl defensively; snap at the child concerned; and sometimes it could even bite the innocent child.

As for the puppy, you need to monitor it also because it could inadvertently injure the kid in the course of play. Other times you just may own an aggressive breed of puppy, which means chances of the puppy injuring the kid are relatively high. That's why it's important to understand your puppy breed as well as its level of activity. If you have a breed that is extra active, the play may be too much or too rough for the child.

Teach them appropriate behavior

As far as relating with a puppy goes, appropriate behavior comprises behaving in a way that does not upset the puppy or make it anxious. If the puppy feels afraid or anxious, or if it feels mishandled, its fighting instincts may be aroused;

wishing to protect itself. For this reason, you need to teach your kid to behave in a friendly manner towards the puppy.

For instance, a puppy or even a fully grown dog will not take it kindly if someone is hovering over it; irrespective of whether it is you or your kid. For that matter, train your child to get into the habit of approaching the puppy from behind or even from the side, and once next to it, to avoid making direct eye contact. And of course, the kid should not hover over the puppy at any time.

It is also good to teach the child that it is important to play in a cool manner when engaging with a puppy; not playing rough, because the puppy may reciprocate by playing even rougher – too rough for the kid. First of all, lifting up the puppy is a no-no for the kid.

Also, to be able to initiate play in a friendly manner or to bring the play to a halt when the child has had enough, it is important that you ensure your puppy is well trained in the commands, come; sit; stay; down; leave it; drop it; and such others that you deem relevant and useful for the circumstance. You don't want the nightmare of trying to control an untrained canine around kids.

Finally in the issue of child behavior, you need to teach your kid what the boundaries are when it comes to puppies – the limit to the body areas the kid can touch the puppy; the type of playing objects it can play introduce to the puppy for play;

and so on. What an adult wouldn't do in regards to a puppy, a kid shouldn't also do. Get the kid to think about times that they want to be alone and play alone; or just rest – if the kid is big enough to understand such communication. Then explain that the puppy needs such alone time too. And even if the kid is much younger, still train it to leave the puppy alone when it shows signs of not wanting to play. In short, train your kid to respect the puppy's personal space.

Reinforce positive puppy and kid behavior

The issue of giving treats to puppies when they behave well has already been explained elsewhere in this book. You need to continue with it whenever you see your puppy playing calmly with your child. Remember you don't have to give big chunks of food as reward – small morsels, preferably your puppy's favorite, will do. And you need to reward your kid too whenever it has had a calm playing session with the puppy; it will reinforce the positive behavior. The reward system and its impact go a long way into strengthening the bond between your kid and the puppy, while creating a safe environment for both of them.

Do not force puppy into kid play

Do all people like playing with kids? No. Likewise, not all dogs like playing with kids even when they are young. If you realize your puppy is not into playing with children, let it be. Respect your puppy's preference. In fact, discourage your kid from playing with that particular puppy, lest you invite aggression.

However, in instances where your puppy shows negative behavior without provocation, only because there happens to be a child in close proximity, there is cause for concern and you need to consult an expert dog trainer or a behaviorist for advice. This is a dangerous situation that requires the input of such professionals. As for you, it is your responsibility to provide your puppy with a safe haven – a place where the puppy can retreat to whenever it feels uncomfortable before children, adults or other dogs; or whenever it feels overwhelmed by things happening around. In this regard, a big enough crate or a comfortable bed will do.

Chapter 18: How to Stop Puppy from Indiscriminate Chewing

Have you witnessed dogs tearing balls open and making tatters of otherwise beautiful toys? Well, puppies and adult dogs can do a lot of mess if not effectively trained. You need to train your puppy not to chew toys, and not to bite into furniture and other things it shouldn't be digging into.

Is chewing entirely strange for puppies?

The straight answer is no. One way puppies learn about their environment is biting or chewing at things it comes across. In fact, we can aptly say that chewing at things is normal for a dog. So a puppy doesn't chew things in a deliberate attempt to destroy them. Rather, it does that because it's only natural for it to do so. Gladly, you can make an effective intervention and train your puppy to keep off toys and other things you consider not right to chew on.

In the meantime, you too have a responsibility to make the environment a deterrent. For example, if you clear from the open area everything you wouldn't want the puppy chewing – like socks; exercise and text books; remote control and such other items; you wouldn't need to worry about the puppy destroying your things. At the same time, you need to guard against sending the puppy mixed signals. You just can't take the old shoe you want to discard and begin playing with it with the puppy, allowing it to chew on it at will. Do you think the puppy is capable of differentiating your brand new sneakers from this old shoe thereafter? You'll have taught it that it's fine to chew on shoes; and so you are bound to have it rough keeping your other pairs safe from the puppy.

Tips to End Puppy's Negative Chewing Behavior

- Identify the items that the puppy likes chewing and put them away into drawers, cabinets, cupboards, and such other places that you can close tightly.

- Introduce your puppy to other activities that can keep it mentally stimulated. That way, you'll divert its attention away from destructive chewing.

- Get your toy some toys that are appropriate for chewing; or those that are referred to as interactive – capable of holding treats within them. When determining the most appropriate toys to buy your puppy, consider if the puppy is an active or occasional chewer because you want a toy that is going to last some reasonable time.

- Train your toy to play with items without chewing them. How do you do that? Easy:

    o Put your puppy on a leash and then throw an item ahead of you. Command the puppy to retrieve the item and once it reaches the item and sniffs at it, you reel the puppy back.
    o Repeat the process until the puppy can pick up the item and bring it back to you as you reel it back.
    o Every time it brings it back, pick the item and throw it again; then command the puppy to retrieve it.
    o Remember to reward the puppy for command well executed.
    o Sooner or later, your puppy will be retrieving items without chewing on them, even when you haven't put the puppy on a leash.

If you are having a serious problem of your puppy chewing on furniture like the kitchen table, spray those places with a substance that is safe but bitter tasting. The puppy will hate the taste and make those things no-chew items.

Conclusion

Now that you understand what Puppy Training entails, you need to take a second look at your puppy, notice the puppy's bad behavior that you have been taking for granted, and see what you can do to correct it. At the same time, you need to re-evaluate the way you handle your puppy, with a view to finding out if there is any unfavorable re-enforcement that you give.

It would also be a good idea for you to go through this *Puppy Training* guide again, particularly if you intend to acquire a new puppy. In fact, after reading through this book and learning how a well trained dog behaves, you'll be in a good position to interview any puppy before you acquire it if you are certain you won't have time to train it at home.

Thereafter, you need to ensure you always have this guide within reach, so that you can use it as reference whenever in doubt about how to handle your puppy in matters of behavior. Besides, it's always good to have some material that can support your explanation when you are advising a friend in matters of puppy training.

Made in the USA
Lexington, KY
25 October 2017